# The Accidental Missionary:
*A Gringo's Love Affair with Peru*

by DAVID BREDEMAN
as told to David L. Winters

The Accidental Missionary: A Gringo's Love Affair with Peru
© **2019**

All rights reserved. No portion of this book may be reproduced, stored in a retrieval system, or transmitted in any form by any means—electronic, mechanical, photocopy, recording, scanning, or other—except for brief quotations in critical reviews or articles, without the prior written permission of the publisher.

Printed in the United States of America by DAVIWIN Publishing
First Printing ISBN: 978-1-7339240-0-9
    Ebook ISBN: 978-1-7339240-1-6

Cover:    JD&J Design, LLC
Interior:  Gary L. Jenkins

All Scripture quotations: Holy Bible, The New King James Version® Copyright © 1982, Thomas Nelson. Used by permission. All rights reserved.

I dedicate this book to the love of my life, my wife Emma. She is the godliest person I know and in thirty years of marriage she has been my greatest inspiration. Thank you Emma for walking the road to Emmaus with me as the Lord's words have burned in our hearts.

—David Bredeman

# Table of Contents

Introduction

| | | |
|---|---|---|
| 1 | Asleep at the Missions Conference | 1 |
| 2 | Dodging the Shining Path and Other Terrors | 17 |
| 3 | A Millionaire Testifies at the Sanhedrin | 35 |
| 4 | Learning Costa Rica and Invading Cuba | 47 |
| 5 | Proposing and Wedding the Peruvian Way | 63 |
| 6 | Jumping Into Peru | 81 |
| 7 | Finding Miraculous Provision Everywhere | 93 |
| 8 | Swashbuckling Through the Jungle | 111 |
| 9 | El Friaje (Without a Jacket) | 125 |
| 10 | Miracles Sustained Us | 131 |
| 11 | Flying Under the Radar with Chicken Campero | 145 |
| 12 | Hunting the Mashco-Piros | 155 |
| 13 | Tipsy in the Spirit | 173 |
| | Epilogue | 181 |

# 1
# Asleep at the Missions Conference

Each January in the 1980s, Christian Assembly Church held a missions conference. Besides displaying the flags of many nations around the sanctuary, members cooked delicious dishes representing various countries, such as Peruvian chicken, Mexican flautas, and French beef bourguignon, just to mention a few. I worked as a carpenter, primarily doing house construction or repair. Though not my passion, carpentry paid the bills while I tried to decide my life's work. After sampling the delicious food and having worked out in cold temperatures most of the day, I settled into a warm, cushy chair to listen.

Though the speakers shared fascinating stories of far-away places, my eyelids grew heavy. As the featured speaker waxed eloquent, I dozed off. Although a giant of the faith, the man's enthusiastic message could not overcome my need for rest. Time passed and I slept soundly. Suddenly, Christian Assembly Pastor Darrel Emmerson interrupted my nap with his booming baritone voice.

"Please stand."

Rousing from my impromptu nap, I figured the sermon had ended. Happy to stand for the benediction, my brain snapped to attention. Ready to go home and get to bed, I jumped to my feet. In an instant, well-meaning church mates swarmed around me, laying hands on me. Their sincere prayers moved me and yet, at the same time, startled me. Spiritual hunger overwhelmed me as I heard their sincere petitions on my behalf. "Amens" and "hallelujahs" punctuated many of their intercessions.

It didn't take long. The content of their prayers clarified that, by standing, I had volunteered to go on the mission field. Inadvertently, I testified to a calling as a missionary.

In First Samuel, chapter three, the Lord visited Samuel at his bedtime to call him into ministry. Could it be God was calling a sleepy head like me? The thought kept rattling around my mind as I sheepishly left the church. In the coming days, I pondered the possibilities.

I later learned what preceded the invitation to stand, the part I hadn't heard, Pastor Darrel said, "If you feel called to the mission field, stand up." On the job the next day, all this weighed on my mind. Although it seemed like a comedy of errors, maybe choosing to become a missionary might be the right path for me.

A short time later, Pastor Darrell spoke publicly of my call into the ministry and specifically into missions. His remarks made it ever more difficult for me to clarify things, particularly as my heart grew conflicted. Could God have orchestrated this mix-up on purpose? Would the Ruler of the Universe call one such as me to become a missionary?

Although I did not comprehend the full implications, God talked to my heart about full-time missions. Apparently, He knew I needed to stand that night. By doing so, He changed my life's course in a matter of minutes.

As the conference continued a few more days, a Wycliffe missionary provided a fascinating slide show. Specifically aimed at young adults, his photos showed a team building something from nothing in the jungle. It caught my attention. The speaker worked with indigenous people in the jungles of Peru. One particular slide showed a bunch of gringos building a hut in the rain forest.

In my heart, I heard God tell me, "Pay attention, this presentation is for you." As an experienced carpenter, I had no doubts I could help with a similar building project. The skills required fit my experience hand-in-glove.

The next day, I requested a meeting with Pastor Darrel. A scholarly seminary graduate, he looked the part to a tee, with prematurely gray hair and neatly-trimmed beard. Although his low and commanding voice could soothe, it unnerved me at this sit-down. He sounded so serious and mature.

"Pastor, thanks for meeting with me," I said.

"David, you've been on my heart throughout the missions conference."

"God is dealing with my heart. I'd like to know more about opportunities for someone like me."

"What do you envision yourself doing on the mission field?"

Pastor listened politely to my comments, appearing unsure of my motivations or sincerity. His doubts might have been even greater if he understood the circumstances of my calling. For years, even after becoming a missionary, Pastor Darrell recalled the determination and fire he saw in my eyes as I stood up that fateful night. Although his description sounded so poetic, years later I finally let him in on my secret. That expression he interpreted as dogged determination represented a sleepy deer in the headlights, not a resolute Christian soldier.

For this important meeting in his office, I let him continue to believe what he might about my calling. I stressed the positive: God's calling on my life grew stronger every day.

Christian Assembly Church supported several ongoing missions around the world. He suggested two of those sites where they needed help. One opportunity involved the Philippines and the other an inner-city church in Lima, Peru. I listened intently to his descriptions of both projects.

"Save your money, David. Working as a missionary is not a vacation and we don't plan to pay your expenses."

As a twenty-four-year-old, new to his church, the Pastor did not know me or understand the depth of my commitment to this new calling. His parting words stuck in my mind, "This will not be a vacation for you. Pray earnestly before going on the mission field. Let's get back together in a week. Tell me what the Lord tells you."

My personality defects do not include excessive introspection. As I left his office, I thought, The Philippines? Nope, way too far away. I am going to Peru.

Although Pastor Darrel had doubts and wanted to see proven character before shelling out the church's money, God kept working in my heart. As far as the choice between the two opportunities, the Philippines held little appeal for me. Having taken Spanish in school, it made more sense to go to a Spanish-speaking country, i.e. Peru. I didn't realize then that a lot people speak English in the Philippines.

As the goal came into focus, I earnestly saved money and tried to prepare myself spiritually.

Within a month or two, the founders of the mission in Lima

came to visit Christian Assembly. Carlos and Celia Estrada rapidly captured my imagination. They sounded positive and upbeat, respecting and accepting me from the outset. My calling to Peru fit with their plans to evangelize South America. Carlos rapidly slid into the role of my mentor and Christian example. A fit, tall, silver-haired 50-something, His dashing visage added ethos to his words. I admired him and particularly the way he treated his wife. His confidence in the Lord and commanding presence made him easy to follow.

"Count on coming for six months or a year," Carlos said. "Bring a sleeping bag and any tools you might need. Get your passport and shots and we will be glad to have you." Darrel had only met the Estrada family once before this trip, and they did not know me from Adam. It's as if I came along at just the right time, as an answer to prayer for workers. Their joy and encouragement buoyed my hope. Stories of God moving in Peru excited my passion to do something meaningful with my life. My heart leapt within me as they told stories of gospel adventures. God orchestrated the timing of the Estrada's visit to coincide with the fever building in me.

The way things worked out reminded me of the Apostle Paul's call into Macedonia, as related in the book of Acts. Paul dreamed of a Macedonian man pleading with him. "Come to Macedonia," the man said. Paul obeyed the call, and the next thing, he found himself in Philippi.

My calling and destination reflected the Lord's grace. The Estradas cherished their calling and their lives as missionaries, having escaped Cuba on one of the last planes out when the Castro regime came to power. First settling in New York City, the Estradas sensed that they belonged on the mission field. Following the Spirit's leading, they started a movement in the early 1960s that resulted in over three hundred churches being planted throughout Peru. By the time I got my unusual call to missions in 1985, the Estradas had long before become fixtures in Peru and the surrounding countries.

Pastor Estrada's vision manifested as a laser focus on winning souls and disciples for Jesus. I became a student of his success. He and Celia showed great resolve during their first twenty-five years of ministry. They overcame major opposition from the Catholic Church establishment and the shamans within various indigenous tribes. In a country where less than 1 percent of the people were evangelicals, he and Celia faced a myriad of challenges when they arrived. He succeeded by harnessing the energy and dedication of youthful followers of Christ. As he had done with many other young adults, he taught me the value of discipline, commitment to the local church, and a growing relationship with Jesus.

Celia Estrada looked the part of a respectable pastor's wife. She projected dignity and warmth that complemented Pastor Carlos's urgency for the gospel and all-business demeanor.

As a country boy from rural Virginia, insecurity fed my apprehension for traveling alone to a foreign country. My grasp of the Spanish language remained rudimentary. Thankfully, Carlos and Celia met me in Miami, and we flew together to Peru. Even with their escort, the adventurousness overwhelmed my senses, excitement pulsed through my body.

*Welcome to Lima*
We arrived early in the morning. Intern students from the Estrada's Bible college swarmed out to the airport to welcome Carlos and Celia back home. The love and fellowship instantly attracted me to those I would soon call friends and fellow laborers. They lived in close fellowship, something new for me. Until I became part of this community, I didn't know how lonely my life had become.

One dark-haired beauty stood near the front of the welcoming party, her presence shone out from the crowd. Emma held hands with one of her girlfriends, a common practice in Peruvian culture then. Looking modest and even borderline disheveled from just getting out of bed, she whispered to her friend in a way that caught my attention.

One of her friends pointed in my direction and said, "Oh, a gringo! I wonder what it would take to win his heart."

"The Lord's will and a lot of patience," Emma told her friend.

Little did she know how prophetic her statement might become. I intended to find out much more about Emma. Of the seventeen students who lived in the church/Bible school complex, she alone spoke fluent English. As I learned more about her, I dreamed of much personal tutoring with my Spanish.

Everything in the new environment and culture awakened my senses and registered strange new feelings. I left Virginia's oppressive July heat and landed in the damp cool breezes of Lima's winter. Since Peru is below the equator, the seasons are reversed from North America. Strong currents flow north from Antarctica and turn the Peruvian coastal waters frigid during wintertime. Disparity between the land temperature and the ocean waters brings ashore a nearly uninterrupted cloud cover. Lima's dull, gray skies suggest rain at any minute, though it often proves an impotent threat. My melancholy temperament did not fit well with the gloomy and dark winter months.

New to the city, the myriad sights and sounds of the bustling metropolis assaulted my senses. Founded by Francisco Pizarro in the 1530s, much of Lima's downtown architecture reflects its long history. The sheer volume of people, traffic and noise in the city overwhelmed this farm boy. Add to that my sketchy language skills. What might happen if I got lost? What if I couldn't find my way back to my host family? The little Spanish I remembered from high school proved inadequate for most situations. This strange new world exhilarated me but frightened me at the same time.

In this challenging phase, the Lord's peace and communion with other Christians became real spiritual nourishment. While amazingly, confusingly new, Lima drove me to a deeper spiritual awakening. Like nothing I had experienced, the love and acceptance of brothers and sisters in the gospel gave me a sense of being home. I lived life wide awake and ready for any adventure. The camaraderie with Bible college students enlivened my experience. These fellow believers, close in age, showed an obvious hunger for the Lord and living out the gospel. We laughed often and enjoyed each other's company.

That isn't to say everything flowed smoothly. The Bible school in Lima enforced strict rules. Intended to make sure that everyone focused on their relationship with God, their code of conduct waxed comprehensive. The staff wasn't running a dating club or a place for finding a spouse. They founded the school to teach devout Christians how to minister. In a Peruvian society that, even then, spiraled toward secularism, their discipline must have appeared antiquated to outsiders. For those within the fellowship, personal purity and learning with few distractions made more sense.

Emma fully bought into the school's mission and zealously followed its rules.

Carlos Estrada not only founded the mission and the school, he served as senior pastor of the now-large church, Catedral de Fe.

He assigned me to stay with a man named Robert Barriger and his family. When we arrived at the Lima airport, Robert greeted the Estradas with much affection. He eventually gravitated in my direction. His friendly manner and compassionate eyes welcomed me into a new world. From the U.S., he spoke fluent English. As we spoke of my plans to occupy their guest room, we both sensed a disconnePPPct. Robert's expectations for my visit differed from my own. He thought

I might stay a week or two. As great of a communicator as Pastor Estrada can be, he did not explain the details of my months-long visit to Lima.

At that moment, Robert responded to me with graciousness, but the look on his face told me something wasn't right. He tried to conceal the surprised look on his face. "Welcome and please excuse me, I need to make a phone call."

Later, I found out Robert and his wife enjoyed a lively conversation regarding the stranger they expected for a week or two who would move in for up to a year. Whatever he said to allay her fears, it must have worked. He drove me to their apartment. I stayed in their three-bedroom home for nine months. I loved the fellowship with Robert, his wife Karyn, and their two small children. Their place became my ideal refuge. The Barrigers taught me much about Lima and Christian fellowship. They served as benevolent guides for my transition to missionary culture.

Although I had just met Emma, my interest in her grew exponentially. Imagine my thoughts when I learned the Barriger's history with her. Years before, when Robert and Karyn arrived in Peru, Emma served as their babysitter. They knew the inside scoop, and I determined to milk them for every detail. Emma became a recurring topic of conversation as I tried to find out as much as I could.

Robert became a huge, positive influence on me. He found the Lord as a 'hippie' surfer on the beaches of Southern California. I suspected his physical appearance had changed little. With light brown hair, a mustache, and a muscular build, he exuded the Southern California surfer persona. His wife stood tallish, blonde, and attractive. They welcomed me as an honored guest, despite the unexpected length of my stay.

Karyn exemplified the best example of a Christian wife and mother. She used her talents wisely in ministry and at home. A great singer, she recorded several worship songs and sold a bunch of CDs through their ministry.

Robert lived in the Bible and tried to practice his faith in every aspect of life. His laid-back manner and gentle spirit made him a great teacher. Their apartment towered seventeen floors above street level. Safe and upscale, this influential part of Lima, called San Isidro, grew on me. With a golf course and shops nearby, it became a picturesque haven after a day of working in the much dingier inner city.

Winter turned to spring: Lima's skies cleared. We could see the Pacific Ocean from their upper-floor apartment. As we ate dinner, amazing sunsets bathed the dining-room in oranges and reds. The days seemed magical and my new friends taught me so much about God and life.

*Insatiable Hunger*

My appetite for all things Peru grew insatiable. Its amazing culture and rich history captivated my intellect and permeated my heart. Karyn, an American by birth, took daily Spanish classes at Lima's Catholic University. I did the same though well behind her in the curriculum. She taught me the bus route to school and to the church where I worked after classes. For my first lesson, I arose bright and early, ready for my first Peruvian adventure! Before we got to the street corner to flag the bus, Karyn gave me a word of advice: "Now you want to remember always to be a considerate gentleman by offering your seat to ladies who board after you," she said.

"Got it," I replied.

We parted and her words kept running through my mind. This is a different culture. Always be a considerate gentleman. As a guy raised in the country, I didn't know city protocol on many issues. Within minutes, I hailed the correct bus and found a seat. Just one block later a well-dressed lady got on the bus. Be a considerate gentleman being my new mantra, I arose and offered her my seat. She gave me a strange look,

# Asleep at the Missions Conference

but accepted and sat down.

That's weird, I thought. She did not appear very appreciative. Didn't she see me being a considerate gentleman? A block or two later, it occurred to me why I had surprised this woman with my gentlemanly gesture; two-thirds of the bus remained empty. One only needs to give up their seat when no other seats are available. I sheepishly learned my first cultural lesson: use common sense when applying axioms regarding Peruvian life.

I took the bus daily from the apartment to the Church, many blocks away in the poorest part of the inner city. God whispered to my heart on these rides. The poor seemed to be everywhere. Their squalid living conditions punctuated their physical and spiritual needs. Jesus opened my eyes and my heart. God taught me His intense love for the poor and His heart for improving their lives. The stark juxtaposition of the Barriger's modern, upscale apartment contrasted to less affluent neighborhoods nearby. God doesn't love anyone an ounce less because of their poverty. Each person counts one in the Father's eyes. Regardless of the world's value system, God's love reaches to all, if only we can use God-inspired vision to see them.

### *Hermano Julian*

The thousand-member Catedral de Fe church became such an inviting place for me. I found Peruvians warm and open to foreigners. Everyone loved and welcomed me with open arms. Well, almost everyone.

Hermano means brother. One of the prominent personalities in Catedral de Fe belonged to Hermano Julian. Although a likable enough man, he reserved judgment on this Johnny-come-lately Gringo carpenter from the United States. My shiny tools notwithstanding, he looked more on the heart than a man's exterior. A carpenter like myself, Hermano

Julian served as leader of the deacons of the church. His role included overseer of any carpentry work or repairs.

The first project Pastor Estrada assigned me involved making a door for the sound booth. "Here is the lumber you will use," Pastor Estrada said. As he spoke, he pointed to a pile of "recycled" wood. These scraps looked as if they had been around since the Spanish Conquest 500 years earlier. My dismay must have shown up on my face. The pastor shot back without delay. "Now, wealth spoils you Americans. You can only work when you have new lumber and power tools," he said. "You will need to adapt to Peruvian ways and a more limited budget."

"Ok," I said with the extent of the meekness I could muster. "Let's see what we've got here." Although the choices underwhelmed me, I found a few pieces that showed promise. The only problem: every time I pulled a piece of wood out of the pile, Julian took the board out of my hands.

"I need to use that piece for something else," he said in Spanish.

I understood enough of the language to get the message, but I could not speak enough to give him a piece of my mind. This turned out for the better.

Hermano Julian's gentle hazing ritual served a key part of my initiation into Peruvian culture. Like a woman who doesn't warm up to a potential suitor right away, the approval of the Country and its people required persistence. They wanted to see the depth of my commitment to them. Despite the challenges, the people won more of my heart every day. When I passed the initiation tests, Peru including Hermano Julian accepted me.

My morning Spanish classes took me to a building fifteen to twenty blocks from the church. After the lessons ended at 10 a.m., I either took the bus or walked to the church. I worked until evening. I loved these strolls through the streets, observing interesting people and so many sights. Street vendors everywhere, they sold food, books, magazines, socks and even underwear. You name it and I could find it at one vendor location or another. God used these prayer walks to change my heart and wake up my mind. Peru needed love, and I wanted to provide it.

The people in Lima include many races and ethnicities. Many trace their roots from one of three regions: The Orient, the Mediterranean or the indigenous Peruvians. Some people had roots in combinations of all three. Most indigenous Peruvians hailed from the mountains or, to a lesser extent, from the jungle. While 84 percent of the country speaks Spanish, the Quechua language is spoken by 13 percent of the population. According to Wikipedia, the constitution of 1993 mandates these two as the official languages of Peru.

Certain people from a European lineage judged native people as uneducated or even less valuable. It broke my heart daily to see Quechua-speaking mothers with their dirty-faced little children sitting on the sidewalks, begging for the smallest amounts of money.

Those early days in Lima provided my first real glimpse into economic and social disparity. Before moving to Peru, I had never even seen a beggar. There aren't many panhandlers in the Shenandoah Valley of Virginia farm country. We had no one asking for money in the streets of our small towns.

Not only did the Quechuas appear poor in material things, they often suffered social humiliation. My heart broke as wealthy passersby treated them as an annoyance or spoke harshly to them. This made me want to give all of my money to each beggar I encountered.

One of my English-speaking friends tried to curb my generosity. "David, you can't give to everyone," he said in a serious tone. "First, you will run out of money. Second, you never know which ones are legitimate. Some of them are just professional beggars."

His words disturbed me. What in the world might lead someone to become a professional beggar? They all appeared in genuine need. My thoughts turned to an age-old question. Do we give because beggars exist? Or, are there beggars because we give? Decades later, this question still creates a dilemma that haunts me.

As Jesus said in three of the four gospels, "For you have the poor with you always, but Me you do not have always" (Matthew 26:11). Why did God choose for me to be born in relative prosperity in the United States? Why was this person or that person born in abject poverty here in Peru? I still don't understand.

Upon seeing with my own eyes, the joy that Jesus brings to people who have so little, the Lord showed me that spiritual poverty is the biggest cause of suffering. Economic poverty, as rough as it can be, is outward and temporary. Spiritual poverty is inward and, without Jesus, eternal. Though Jesus can make poor people happy, without Him, even the rich can be miserable. I could not cure all of Peru's financial ills. I came to bring Jesus. My target would be: reverse spiritual poverty in those I met.

*Spanish Eggs*
The Spanish language became a constant struggle during those first nine months. No matter how smart (you think) you are, living in a country where you don't understand the language becomes humbling. Even a three-year-old looks smarter in comparison. What's terrible is when someone speaks and you fake your way through it. Then, they ask you a question, only to realize that you have not tracked with a word they said for the last ten minutes.

I put my heart into learning and growing in knowledge of my adopted home. One day Karyn Barriger put me to the

## Asleep at the Missions Conference

test. She asked me to go to the store and buy eggs.

"OK," I said. "Remind me, how do you say eggs?"

"Well, you go into the store and if you see none you ask, ¿Tiene huevos?, which means do you have eggs?"

My new mission excited me. Operation: egg procurement! I prepared myself to go to the store and buy something we actually needed. Look out, Peru. Here I come.

The word tiene comes from the verb 'tener' which means to have. My goal appeared readily achievable. I'd mastered this word. All I had to do: remember the word huevos. The elevator empty, I repeated huevos, huevos, huevos. Sounds easy, I thought. A man on a quest, I strutted out the lobby door with rugged determination. You have got this. I smiled at those I met along the way. Like a real adult, I made my way with purpose to local market. But somehow, along the way, my huevos, huevos, huevos, turned into huesos, huesos, huesos.

The relatively small store reminded me of a small, corner market back home. My eyes scanned the few aisles. No eggs jumped out at me.

"¿Tiene huesos?" I asked, beaming with confidence.

"¿De res o de chancho?" the lady behind the counter responded.

Wait a minute, I think to myself. I have no clue what res means. Was res the word for beef? Chancho means pig. Confronted with two words that held no meaning for me, I sensed that whatever I asked for had nothing to do with eggs! My only response: blurt out, no gracias and hurry out the door empty-handed. The clerk looked at me as one who might be an idiot or perhaps mentally ill. Later and after further reflection, it occurred to me that instead of asking for eggs, I had asked for bones. The first practical test of my budding Spanish language skills resulted in a total fail. We ate cereal that morning.

# **Dodging The Shining Path and Other Terrors**

In 1985, a terrorist group called The Shining Path wreaked havoc in many corners of the country. This communist movement hated all things Western, capitalist, financial, etc. Their strategy involved destabilizing the country, hoping to overthrow the pro-Western government and replace it with a leftist one. Peruvian history left many open wounds, often exploited by those seeking power or influence.

In 1530, the Spanish defeated the Inca Empire. A mostly peaceful people, the Incas proved unprepared for the advanced weapons and the brutality of the conquistadors. Today, nearly 50 percent of the Peruvian population claim lineage from the Incas. Many of them still speak Quechua, the language of the Incas. Per Quechua lore, the Inca Empire will rise again and defeat their former conquerors.

The communists astutely exploited this Quechua legend, trying to sway the indigenous population to revolt and make this ancient prophecy come true. The Shining Path goal of overthrowing the Peruvian government caught the attention of the ruling powers. As we swept through our daily routines, we often saw signs of The Shining Path destruction or government actions aimed at combatting them.

The Shining Path regularly planted car bombs in Lima and created havoc with mass killings in the countryside. In 1985, the Barrigers and I routinely awoke in the night to loud explosions near our apartment. The threat of terrorism and societal unrest made for dangerous times in Lima. For a while, the city became known as the second most dangerous city in the world after Beirut, Lebanon.

The government responded by seizing assets and making it hard to import and export goods. By controlling the flow of currency, they hoped to choke off the terrorist's resources. As an unintended consequence, large companies fled Peru. This disrupted daily life as the value of Peruvian money, the sol, deflated daily. As a defense mechanism, people with money tried to exchange it for foreign currency, mainly U.S. dollars.

Again, the government took measures to control or at least slow the volatility. They made it illegal for Peruvians to own dollars or use them within Peru. This added a layer of complexity for me and other short-term missionaries. Add the mass killings by terrorism and the era became a challenging one for missionaries and other foreigners in Peru ... unless you enjoy being broke and in danger.

Politically, Peru's leaders claimed the country remained a democracy. Several military coups and dictatorships later, the rest of the world wasn't so sure. By the time I arrived in Lima, Peru found itself recovering from a nationalistic movement that triggered unrest and brought strong reprisals from the military. To fight the tide of rising violence, the police enforced a curfew of nine in the evening. Only police or military were supposed to occupy the streets between 9:00 p.m. and 6:00 a.m.

On one particularly dark night, the curfew descended while I remained a good distance from the apartment. I hurried home furtively, trying to make it to the safety of the Barriger home. As church bells tolled nine, I took several shortcuts through darkened side streets. Suddenly, an eerie sensation crept up my back; I was not alone. My eyes danced back and forth, detecting men hiding behind trees and around corners. By the dim light, I spied large guns jutting from the shadows. Were the men police or military? Or were they terrorists swooping in for a random attack? Or perhaps the shadows cloaked guys such as me, finding themselves caught outside after curfew.

I blistered the pavement trying to hurry home. Full-out running might attract the wrong type of attention, so I hustled with the exaggerated strides of an elite athlete competing in an Olympic speed-walking event. To my relief, the apartment came into view before any police nabbed me or terrorists filled me with bullets. The next day, I learned that the Peruvian Army received a tip that terrorists were planning an attack nearby. Soldiers? Terrorists? What mattered is that God protected me, and I arrived safely home.

### *Visa Gymnastics*

Under Peruvian immigration regulations, I carried a visitor's visa. Although my plan included a nine-month stay, the terms of the tourist visa meant I must leave Peru every three months. Afterwards, the rules allowed me to re-enter the country. My hosts explained that my absences needn't be long or involve going back to the United States. A short visit to a neighboring country for an afternoon sufficed—music to my ears. I smiled for two days envisioning the chance to get out of the big city and see the Peruvian countryside.

Lima is the second largest desert city in the world, after Cairo, Egypt. The climate and other urban challenges prevent it from being the prettiest place (sorry friends from Lima). But what it might lack in architectural splendor, it makes up for in heart. Even with its many charms, this country boy longed for a respite from the congestion and hoped to meet people from the more rural areas.

Our church arranged a large conference in the southern Peru town of Tacna, near the Chilean border. Several of us traveled along to take part in ministry. We planned to support our church pastors as they taught, pray and to be helpful in whatever ways presented themselves. Eager to get out of the large city and stay on the up and up with the Peruvian government, the trip excited me. Once there, we thoroughly enjoyed the church people and jumped right in by helping at the conference.

While in Tacna and sensing a break in the flow of the meetings, my friend Pastor Alfredo and I made our way across the border. The Chilean officials smiled and stamped my passport. After they politely granted my request, Alfredo and I snapped a few pictures, ate Chilean empanadas, and bid the country adios. The whole task took thirty minutes. This short visit made me good for another three months of ministry in Peru. After the conference, I returned to Lima refreshed in spirit and affirmed in my official visitor status.

With my visa renewed, I poured myself into the carpentry and other jobs at the mission. Accomplishments and camaraderie fed my soul. The progress on the physical building encouraged everyone. I enjoyed using various kinds of exotic woods unknown to me. My early successes led to hope for a future in this missionary thing.

As I learned more Spanish, my grasp of Peruvian humor increased, and the nuances of culture dawned on me. It did not take long to realize that the Lord used my carpentry skills to get me onto the mission field but intended for me to branch out. My interest in ministry activities grew as I saw others reaching out to the unchurched. God stirred my heart in prayer times, and His Word suggested much more in store for me, both to learn and to do. What if God's purposes for me included direct ministry through speaking, praying and loving people?

*Emma on My Mind*
While my days were chock-full of carpentry and conversations in Spanish, something else increasingly captured my attention. My language skills improved at a healthy clip as my admiration for Emma grew. Although we spent no time alone together, I focused on her at church services and when we socialized in groups.

Each day, I ate lunch (and sometimes dinner) in the cramped little dining nook on the roof of the church. As college students, we enjoyed simple meals of beans, rice and chicken. A dear woman named Hermana (Sister) Celinda cooked our meals. She lovingly plated the food and placed it on our tables. Hermana Celinda became a mother figure, always praying for and comforting us. She cooked amazing meals, using the meager resources provided to her.

The exception to the usual menu came when parishioners donated food to the school. For example, someone gave us two large barrels of mushrooms. Sister Celinda magically concocted many tasty dishes before these ingredients rotted or spoiled.

Once a week, a church member, who owned a chicken carry-out place, donated the chicken heads to the school.

Talk about a fowl surprise! Imagine the first time I settled into my usual place at the rooftop dining table to see soup with a decapitated chicken head staring back at me. I kept my composure, but just barely. Knowing the menu, Emma found a place setting where only soup occupied her bowl. No chicken head for her. Smart lady.

I watched Emma's interactions with her classmates and enjoyed her peaceful spirit. She exuded grace and innocence. She charmed me. Intelligent, she came across as capable and even-keeled. Although we seldom spoke directly, my attachment grew strong over the next three months as I thought about her often throughout the day.

During this span, I began to understand the gulf between the Mestizos and the indigenous people. Mestizos, those of Spanish descent, have long held economic control in Peru. They populate the large city of Lima and earn higher wages than most of the Quechua people living in the countryside. Some of Emma's relatives came from the Quechua and it made me all the more curious about tribesmen and Inca descendants.

On one of my first trips into the jungle, I lay in my one-man tent thinking about the history of this amazing land. Standard procedure, I strung mosquito netting from along the ceiling of the little tent. It is imperative not to touch the netting itself because mosquitoes can sting through the netting even though their bodies won't fit through the tiny holes.

God worked on my heart as I lay there listening to the jungle sounds in the night. These people needed salvation, and I wondered if I could help. My thoughts turned often to their need for God's love and daily presence. I knew love's power to eradicate their many fears.

Eaten alive by bugs earlier in the day, my body suffered tremendously. A brief wash in the muddy river helped for an hour or so, but soon the creepy, crawly sensations enveloped my skin. A distant howler monkey proclaimed an eerie warning, and a four-legged animal stalked back and forth outside my tent, silhouetted by the bright moonlight.

In those difficult conditions, I experienced the greatest joy of my life to that point. My adventures released endorphins, feeding inner needs previously unnamed. Here I lay, a farm kid and a woodworker from Virginia's Shenandoah Valley, camping out in the Amazon jungle with people who only spoke Spanish. Feeling wild and free, my heart soared.

*North to Ecuador*
Days turned into weeks, and it became time to renew my visa for the last three months of my visit. This time, I hoped to travel north to Ecuador. My vision for the trip included fresh vistas, interesting new people, and unique adventures. After discussing it with my host, Pastor Robert suggested I go with him to a conference in Tumbes. Then I could take a detour on the way back and travel to Huaquillas, just across the border in Ecuador.

Before Tumbes, Robert and I went by bus to a city in the Andes Mountains called Cajamarca. Robert ministered at a local church. While he took the lead, I planned to study how he interacted with the locals and to pitch in praying for people.

Cajamarca boasts a rich history. It is where the Inca king, Atahualpa surrendered to invading Spaniards. Once captured, the king promised to fill a large room with gold twice and silver once, if they promised not to kill him. The greedy conquistadors agreed to his terms.

Atahualpa's people scoured the countryside to meet their invader's demands and save their ruler. The Incas stockpiled precious metals in caves and natural crevices. As soon as the Incas filled the room three times, the Spanish soldiers dragged their king to the city square. The Conquistadors mercilessly executed Atahualpa. The episode proved an unholy beginning to a sad future for the Quechua people and a brutal end to the Inca Empire.

History aside, the three-day church conference in Cajamarca became a smashing success. Many people received help and teaching that led to several first-time decisions for Christ. I felt deliriously happy to know of my part in seeing people accept Jesus as Savior and Lord. If I hadn't been convinced up to this point, I now knew that the missionary life included great emotional rewards. With the whole church wishing us a fond farewell, we boarded our bus for the overnight trip back toward the coast.

At midnight, the bus came to a loud and grinding halt. In the commotion, most of the passengers woke up and looked around the cabin. Minutes later, and a few at a time, we all exited the bus. Once outside, we overheard the driver tell his back-up driver, "It looks like a worn-out wheel bearing. If so, the repair will take a while."

"Oh well," Robert said. "Let's climb back aboard and get more shuteye."

"I understand," I said. "Not many options out here."

By this time, I learned to accept delays as just part of the culture and infrastructure. It did no good to become impatient or complain. Robert climbed back onto the bus and settled in for a nap. Those long trips tired me out, and I learned to sleep in most circumstances and positions.

Hours later, a bee buzzed in my face, waking me. Once I shooed the intruder away and got my bearings, something made me sit up and look around the bus.

"Robert, wake up," I shouted.

"What's the matter," he said, his eyes still drowsy. "I was sleeping soundly."

"Everyone has gone! Where did they go?"

Robert scratched his head, still regaining consciousness.

"They must have hitched rides into the next town. Let's get out and look around."

We exited the large vehicle to see the driver still working away with grease up to his armpits.

"He doesn't look near finishing," Robert said. "Look at all those bus parts on the ground."

We exchanged glances as we considered our situation.

"Would you open the baggage compartment?" I asked the back-up driver, who stood nearby. Up to this point, I had maintained my composure. Now, my anger rose to the surface. The drivers must have known we had been sawing logs. Why didn't they wake us to get a ride before the hour grew so late?

"Yeah, yeah, give me a minute," he said in a disgusted tone.

Twenty minutes passed with no sign of the back-up driver moving a muscle. He stood there with nothing to do. I became irritated at seeing him idly standing there when he could have been helping us. Although my momma taught me good manners, sleep deprivation washed away her guidance. I stomped back toward the bus. Robert followed me and realized I had an idea. Soon, I climbed aboard and located the key to the baggage compartment.

We exited and stealthily slipped around the side of the giant vehicle. Using the key, I gained entry, retrieving Robert's and then my luggage. Just as I set our bags on the roadside, the now-alert and suddenly mobile back-up driver rounded the side of the bus.

"Stop!" he shouted. "You mustn't get in there! You don't have permission!"

Robert and I ignored him. I left the key in the lock, and we dragged our bags out to the side of the road, planning to hitch a ride.

"Robert, the whole time we had been waiting for the back-up driver to get our bags, a steady stream of traffic passed us. We might have hitched a ride with any one of them to get to the next coastal town."

"And now, with bags in hand and ready to go, the constant stream of traffic ceased," Robert said. "Not a single car in the distance. It's as if they closed the road?"

If they had crickets in this part of Peru, they might have broken the ghostly silence. After an eternity of no traffic, both the driver and his assistant teased us.

"It looks like I am almost done with the repairs and we can be on our way," the driver said.

"Let's leave these impatient men out here," the back-up driver said, forcing a laugh. "Good eating for the condors."

"Yep," the driver exclaimed, "tomorrow we'll drive back only to see gringo bones and fat condors!" Both men shrieked with laughter. They thought our predicament funny, but Robert and I did not see the levity. We just glanced at each other and kept staring down the road.

We needed to make our escape before the back-up driver took further action. Although I was not sure what he might do, my nerves jangled. Perhaps the cranky assistant might wrestle Robert and me for our bags and forcibly put them back on the bus.

Instead we prayed, "Lord, get us out of here, please." After a quick amen, we spied one lone truck coming around the bend in the distance. His truck rumbled up to us and stopped with a muted squealing sound. The man stopped and collected us. He saved us from the hungry condors! The Scripture came to mind: "I will call upon the Lord, who is worthy to be praised; So shall I be saved from my enemies" (Psalm 18:3).

Once we made it to the coast, Pastor Robert informed me he needed to head south to Lima. He showed me where I should board to go north toward Ecuador. In a flash, he boarded the next bus, leaving me alone at the curb by the bus terminal. Not two minutes later, a familiar-looking bus approached. As it got close, I recognized our earlier driver and back-up driver. Ducking behind a post, they thankfully must not have seen me.

Although worn out, I boarded a different bus about an hour later. By this point, my tiredness level registered off the charts. If we kept to the schedule, the bus would arrive near the northern border at 9:00 a.m. the next morning. I rolled up my jacket and used it as a cushion against the vibrating window. I slept soundly as we bumped along the rough road.

When I awoke, I found myself in Tumbes. The bus rumbled to a stop at a desolate outpost. My mind flooded with images and feelings not unlike an old Western movie. Because of our exchange with the other bus drivers, I cautiously stepped off the bus and onto the dirt road. No one waited for me. The only person to get off at this stop, I felt lonely as I surveyed the few deserted shops and lone gas station. As the bus drove off, I oriented myself and walked three blocks to the address Robert had written on a small piece of paper.

"Greetings, Senor. Buenos días. I am David Bredeman. Pastor Estrada told you to expect me, I believe."

"Yes, David, welcome," Pastor Mario answered in English. Tall, thin, and affable, his smile and bear hug made me feel most welcome. One of the first missionaries sent out from Lima by the Estradas, Mario earned a reputation for hard work and dedication. His warm personal manner lit up his home. I followed him into his house and deposited my duffle bag in a corner. The place looked spotless and tidy.

"How are things going?" I asked, trying to start small talk. Sweat poured from my brow in response to the equatorial heat. When alone, the perspiration wasn't a big deal, but now, trying to make a good impression, it weighed on my mind. Every part of my body oozed sweat after the short walk. I felt like a self-conscious, drowned rat. So much for wowing them in the hinterlands.

Pastor Mario introduced me to his polite family, and they listened intently to my story and my reason for being there. I started to feel more comfortable. Not long after the greetings, my host handed me a napkin. Although a kind gesture, I realized my Niagara Falls of sweat had become the center of everyone's attention.

"I need to renew my visa," I said. What I did not say: I can't wait to hop on the bus to the cooler climate of Lima later this evening.

*Aguas Verdes (Green Waters)*
After our visit, Mario and I traveled back to the bus stop for our half-hour trip to the Peruvian border town of Aguas Verdes, which means "green waters" in English. The countryside intrigued me. Lots of vegetation and simple housing lined the two-lane road. Once at our destination, we took the short walk across a combination automobile/pedestrian bridge into Ecuador.

Although the bridge marked the border, I saw only a small sign welcoming us to Ecuador. I expected more formality. No guards or gates slowed traffic or checked pedestrians as they poured over the bridge. Huge bugs fluttered near us as we crossed the putrid-smelling water. Fumes from the diesel trucks filled the air and made it even harder to breathe in the oven-like conditions.

"There's the immigration office over there," Mario said, pointing to a small building. The immigration office sat by the side of the road five hundred yards from the bridge.

I entered the spartan-looking office and proceeded to the short line. Pastor Mario stood nearby to bolster my still less-than-fluent Spanish, if needed. I waited only a few minutes.

In Spanish, I greeted the men behind the counter and explained that I needed my visa renewed. A gruff-looking Ecuadorian eyed my passport, then glanced back at me.

His furrowed brow and thin mustache unsettled me. I scanned the room, my eyes adjusting from the bright sunshine to the room dimly lit by fluorescent bulbs. Asbestos tile on the floors, yellowed from decades of inadequate cleaning, lent the place a dingy mood. The vibe and the stares of immigration police made me feel like a dog on the verge of taking his monthly bath. I wanted out as soon as possible. God, are you listening up there? An armed guard near the door did little to comfort me. I considered making a run for it.

After staring at my visa for a few moments, the immigration official dashed my hopes of a quick departure. "You are to stay in Ecuador for two days, and only then you may leave the country. And don't you dare cross that bridge back into Peru for forty-eight hours!"

"Yes, sir. I understand, sir." I shifted my feet and looked back at Pastor Mario, who looked worried on my behalf.

To add insult to injury, the official wrote "48 hours" on my old visa, which signaled to the world I must stay in Ecuador for two days. As I tried to process this latest development, the heat pulsed through my brain. Two days sounded like an unbearable sentence in the sweltering weather. What would I do? I knew no one in Ecuador. Would I have to sleep out on a park bench? Could I get jail time for loitering in Ecuador?

Outside the customs station, Pastor Mario looked downcast. "David, this is very bad news. I must get back to Tumbes. We have church tonight and I lead the service. I can't stay here with you in Ecuador."

"That's okay; I understand." My voice trembled like a forlorn orphan on the streets of New York City. No doubt my face betrayed mild panic at the thought of spending two days alone in this intimidating little town.

"Where should I camp out?" Having no money, it hardly mattered that I saw no Holiday Inn around. This small town probably didn't have any overnight lodging. Where would I sleep? How could I pass the time? The mammoth bugs we saw on the bridge might eat me alive.

"Don't worry, David. I know a friend who you can stay with for two days. You might find his place rustic, but they are a loving, Christian couple. They pastor a church in Aguas Verdes."

Relief flooded over me. Pastor Mario didn't plan to abandon me to the streets. "That sounds just great," I said. "Rustic is my middle name. I grew up in the country."

"There is one complication," Pastor Mario said. "My friend lives on the Peruvian side of the bridge!"

Pastor Mario smiled as his eyes filled with mischief. Although no one questioned us when we crossed the bridge earlier, the immigration checkpoint sat in a direct line of sight to the bridge. If the immigration officials caught me, they might throw me into an Ecuadorian hoosegow. Imagine the headline: "Short, but Promising Missionary Career Ends in Disgrace!" My blood pressure pulsed in the right side of my brain.

We waited ten minutes and joined a pack of four men who appeared to be traveling together. Gasping in air, my body heaved as we walked along. No one from the immigration office noticed as I sneaked back across the bridge. For two days, I planned to hide out as an illegal alien in Peru.

Sometimes, border towns get a bum rap because of crime or other problems. Aguas Verdes, while not the prettiest place, lived up to its name meaning "green waters." Their founding fathers built the little metropolis on a swamp. Platform houses rose above standing, putrefying water. The whole town stinks. I remember wondering if the oppressive heat and humidity of this place might kill me. Perhaps because of the smell or the complexity of building houses on stilts, the town remained small. The whole village shared one sit-down bathroom, meaning everyone either used it or otherwise made do. This no doubt added to the unusual fragrance of the place.

My hosts tried to be as friendly as possible. Unlike Pastor Mario, they had no notice of my visit. Their Christian love shone through the circumstances, and they graciously let me stay. Despite their hospitality, we had trouble communicating. Though they spoke only Spanish, and I almost spoke Spanish, we barely understood each other. I caught parts of their conversations, a word here or there. After fifteen minutes, the lack of depth in my Spanish vocabulary made for awkward moments of silence and numerous blank looks.

Mosquitoes buzzed, torturing man and beast. The possibility of malaria and yellow fever crossed my mind.

Though Pastor Mario and I had walked across the bridge both ways between countries, most people drove over in their cars. As I soon learned, the steady traffic continued day and night past our stilt-assisted perch. Since Ecuadorians and Peruvians did not need permission to cross the border, no one stopped their cars or checked papers along this main road. The noise level made difficult sleeping conditions even worse. It made me wonder how the Apostle Paul stayed so happy all the time. As a spoiled American, I longed for my comfortable bed and cooler weather back in Lima. Travel became one of the hardest parts of being a missionary. As I later learned, God's Spirit sustains us as we minister. The big challenges arise when the excitement wanes.

The sun rose on what promised to be a long, miserable day. My adorable Christian hosts did their best. They spoke no English, and tried hand motions to make me understand. Without the ability to say much, the two days dragged. As a pastime, I stared through the floorboards of their house into the murky, green waters below. My mind envisioned man-eating snakes, caimans and worse.

Sheets of corrugated steel comprised the walls of the house. Each panel included holes in it, which added only a small amount of ventilation. Environmentalists can attest that poverty benefits the earth. Those with no money know much about recycling. The highlight of my visit came as I peered through a hole in one of the steel walls. The neighbor's television offered a distraction from the heat. They watched an old cartoon, "The Flintstones." Fred and Barney gave me a small piece of home and eased my loneliness. The voices dubbed in Spanish did not fit my recollection of the characters, but I didn't care. Bedrock took me away from my circumstances for an hour or so.

When not watching the neighbor's television, the three small children of my host family stared up at me with big, brown eyes. They captured my heart with their pleasant smiles and endless curiosity. My visit must have been an extreme oddity, like a spaceman landing from Mars. Plenty of backpacking, gringo tourists crossed their little border bridge, but none stopped to live on their dining room floor for two nights. I acted out my answers to their questions as best I understood them.

The family ate beans and rice three times a day for the two days of my visit. I felt humbled to the core by their simple hospitality and willingness to share with a stranger. With the Barrigers, I had grown accustomed to eating meat and potatoes with every meal. Most Peruvians in the countryside eat more rice than meat for obvious economic reasons.

As I sat staring at my third or fourth straight meal of beans and rice, my mind wandered to life growing up in Virginia. Mom served rice once a month when she made Chinese food. Oh, for a burger and fries! Or maybe one of my mother's home-cooked meals. Rice grows in abundance in huge fields in the northern part of Peru. It provides a staple of the diet of people throughout the country because of its accessibility and low cost.

I tried to have little conversations with my host family, but most of these attempts fell flat. Time dragged. The sparsely furnished home and the risks of going outside made me feel like a prisoner. I paced back and forth.

At last, with my departure time only thirty minutes away, I grew eager to bid my host family farewell and to thank them for their extreme kindness. Without them, a park bench might have my name on it.

They insisted I not leave on an empty stomach and served up one more meal. After two days of beans and rice, morning, noon, and night, I yearned to get back to Tumbes for fried chicken. As I sat down at the simple wooden table, here came a double serving of beans and rice. Knowing how great the sacrifice for them to share their meager food rations, refusing was not an option. Though I tried to hide my feelings, consuming the beans and rice became a sacrifice for me. My digestive track must have expanded to twice its normal size, generating cramps like I'd never felt before.

Thinking of the town's only bathroom, I launched into the first bite. As I surveyed my plate and my stomach rumbled, the pastor and his wife left the table for another part of their little home. Just then, a neighbor's chihuahua wandered through the open door. The pooch looked up at me as if to say, "Hey Buddy, what do you have there?" Perhaps deliverance had arrived on four legs.

The dog certainly looked hungry. I decided not to let this golden opportunity pass me by, so I dropped a large spoonful of the food near him. If it worked, perhaps I could divest twenty percent of my meal. I stared at the thin-looking dog. To my great surprise, the chihuahua looked contemptuously at the food. Then, that finicky pooch strutted off, tail held high.

What now? I had no plan to put the food back on my plate. I did the only available thing; I smooshed the rice between the floorboards with my foot. I hoped to see it fall harmlessly into the green waters below without detection by my hosts. If my plan worked, my ingratitude might go unnoticed and a caiman would take in a few extra carbohydrates. Not my finest moment as a missionary, but more beans and rice looked like a mountain my body could not climb. My luck continued to run from terrible to worse. The food lodged between the floorboards of the house.

After consuming the rest of my meal, I thanked the couple for their kindness in opening their home and their hearts to a stranger in distress. The pastor walked me back toward the border crossing, but first wanted us to stop in a specific leather store. He knew the shopkeeper and conversed with him in Spanish while I browsed the merchandise.

The retailer asked my host, "Does he speak Spanish?"

My host took my pride down another notch when he responded with a twinge of disgust on his face, "Not much."

I got over it as soon as the bus to Tumbes pulled away, my fresh new visa affixed to my passport. That evening the most magical fried chicken graced my plate. Yes, hold the beans and rice please!

# 3

# A Millionaire Testifies at the Sanhedrin

With inflation devaluing the Peruvian currency, before long a million soles were valued at just sixty dollars in U.S. currency. Although exhilarated to be a millionaire—at least in Peruvian currency—the buying potential remained modest. Alfredo Herrera, a young, single pastor at our church in Lima and I embarked on a trip through the Andes to a city called Cuzco. We had become good buddies and spent many hours together. Alfredo taught classes as a professor in the Bible college. Being one of Emma's teachers, he knew her well and understood the school's code of conduct. Sometimes I shared with him my admiration for one of his students. He dutifully reminded me of the student rules of conduct and prohibition against dating. As a friend and brother in the Lord, he sympathized but also respected the status quo.

Alfredo hadn't been to Cuzco in a long time and felt excited to share the experience with someone so interested in its amazing history. Cuzco is the longest continuously inhabited city in the Americas. It served as the capital of the Incas and remains surrounded by amazing Inca ruins. Off we went on our trip, and my expectations grew as we took the long bus rides over the mountains.

Pastor Alfredo taught me many things on the long ride, some historical about Peru and some about Christian living. His commitment to reaching the lost for Jesus inspired and energized me. Having a strong Quechua heritage, he had high cheekbones, darker skin. and the signature crook of his nose. Dark eyes flashed as he vividly told stories, fascinating me and taking my mind off the long travel time.

The mystery of how the Incas cut and moved giant stones captivated me. Alfredo prepped me well for touring the ancient ruins. The Incas had not discovered the wheel before building their stone cities, nor did they understand how to make steel. Yet they carved and moved huge stone slabs into place with precision. So precise their measurements that hundreds of years and many earthquakes later, you still cannot slip even a piece of paper between the joints of the large stones.

Modern-day Cuzco is infamous for its plentiful and artful pickpockets. As a novice missionary back then, no one described me as the savviest of world travelers. On this trip, I made the mistake of wearing army pants with loose pockets that hung open. When I prepared for our day in Cuzco, the faint voice of the Holy Spirit whispered to me, suggesting that I put a million soles in my shoe. I did so and put the other million soles in my pants pocket.

# A Millionaire Testifies at the Sanhedrin

While in Cuzco, Alfredo and I had a few days between our arrival and our first church meeting. He suggested we play tourist and make our way to Machu Picchu, a train ride away from the city. The most famous of Inca ruins, many consider it a must-see on their bucket lists.

When we got to the train station, throngs of people buzzed around us. Most indigenous Cuzco residents measured a foot shorter than the average person from the USA. I stuck out like a lighthouse on a foggy night. If thieves lurked nearby, they must have smelled my inexperience. Anxiety welled up in me while we waited for the train. My overnight bag held all of our travel documents and itinerary information. I slung the strap of my bag over my shoulder for added protection.

I kept my hands in my pockets, trying to ward off anyone with nefarious motives. As the train approached, everyone moved at once. The noise of the train deafening; the heat and the crowd added to the disorienting effect. When jockeying to board the train, I dodged little people darting in and out, trying to get ahead of us.

My bag danced on top of people's heads as they pushed and shoved to get by. With the potential for either losing my bag or getting my neck jerked from my body, I reached out to grab the bag and held it tight against my body with both hands.

After the worst of the hustle and bustle passed, I plunged my hands back in my pockets to find them both empty! I looked around; no one made eye contact. My accusing gaze darted back and forth, but to no avail. A sinking feeling came over me as I realized what had just happened. Someone stole a million soles from me. How foolish was I for being such an easy mark!

Alfredo looked back at me as we neared the boarding stairs. He noticed the distressed look on my face. "What's wrong?" he asked.

I was speechless. Not a single word in English or Spanish came to mind. The only thing I could do was to dejectedly pat both empty pockets and tilt my head to the side. My friend's sympathetic head nod acknowledged my dismay.

Thanks to the prompting of the Holy Spirit, I still had the million soles hidden in my shoe. Feeling less a millionaire and more like an inexperienced tourist, I climbed aboard the train.

The joy escaped our pleasure trip like a teakettle blowing off steam. Primitive seats on the decrepit passenger car redefined hard. They felt even more uncomfortable after being robbed. I learned that mountain people did not bathe as often as city folks. In the developed world, we enjoy hot water on demand in our cozy, climate-controlled homes. Not the case in the high Andes of those days. Understandably, any of us might delay the rigors of ice water baths in a freezing house. The lack of readily available hot water also affected the frequency of washing clothes. Hand-washing your wardrobe in large tubs must have been a cumbersome chore. Most people rarely did laundry. As we passed through the breathtaking countryside, the sting of being robbed remained hard to shake. Overall, it made for a sad and stinky ride to Machu Picchu.

Once at the Lost City of the Incas, I forgot my woes and drank in one of the most fascinating places in the world. Machu Picchu lies hidden atop a mountainside, closed to the outside world until re-discovered in 1911. Since then, it has been named one of the Seven New Wonders of the World. Amazing and well worth losing a million soles over, we thrilled to view a kaleidoscope of interesting vistas. Much of the structures used by the ancient society have endured, undisturbed.

Formed in the fifteenth century, Machu Picchu sits 7,970 feet above sea level. Pastor Alfredo and I labored climbing around and through the fascinating structures. By the time of our visit in the mid-1980s, massive reconstruction activities had rebuilt several of the outlying buildings. I easily pictured the place teeming with Incas, strolling around the royal estate or working terraced farmland on the hillsides.

With most of the vegetation trimmed back, I was stunned by the intricacy of Machu Picchu. The arches fascinated me. Most doorways included a narrowing at the top, then a flat lentil. This construction held the heavy stones in place despite frequent seismic shifts over the centuries. Though the stone structures in Cuzco are larger, some the size of a Volkswagen car, Machu Picchu gripped me more dramatically because of its location on the mountaintop.

"What's that peak over there?" I asked. "The view is calling to me."

"That's Wayna Picchu, which means little brother," Alfredo said. "We have plenty of time before the train heads back to Cuzco. Come on."

I excitedly followed Alfredo down into the valley, then started up the other side. We ascended with difficulty, breathing the thin air and negotiating the steep grade. For a few moments along the way, we wondered if we would make it to the top. Although in good physical health, we remarked that our lungs had never balked to this degree. Slowly and carefully, we followed the trail to the top.

Once at the summit, the view proved worth our trouble. When we first arrived at the peak, we peered into the distance, a view of many kilometers. Most of the surrounding mountains sported snowcaps. Below rocky hills gave way to verdant valleys. Most spectacular, the vista of Machu Picchu defies adequate description. The whole adventure provided food for the soul and spirit.

Before we descended back down to the bus stop, clouds rolled in. In a few minutes, they obscured our view. It happened quickly. As we started down, we could see nothing beyond a few feet in front of us. The panoramic views disappeared, replaced by a haunting fog. I found Machu Picchu stunning, glorious, and complex.

We traveled back on the same train, our hearts filled with wonder and images of Peru's distant past civilization. Unlike the sadness of just being robbed, we smiled and laughed recalling the joy of the day.

"That must have been one of the most incredible things I've ever seen," I said.

"Their ingenuity blows me away," Alfredo said.

"How did they move those giant stones and set them in the precise place?"

Alfredo just shook his head and peered out the train window at the setting sun. No more words came, and we traveled along, feasting on what we'd seen.

Back in Cuzco, we visited various churches and enjoyed the fellowship of other believers along the way. Our goals included ministering to local pastors and encouraging Christians in their daily walk with the Lord. As we taught, the awesome presence of God descended in these remote places. Our hearts filled up with joy as we worshipped Jehovah and prayed with the sweet people there. I stood amazed at God's love one more time. His ability to meet human needs, regardless of the place or time, still warms my soul.

Ironically, we learned that we could have taken a tourist train to Machu Picchu, which would have been much safer. Chances are I could have avoided getting my money stolen. Oh well. Good to remember the next time I am in Cuzco.

The main purpose of our trip fulfilled, Alfredo, and I prepared to return to Lima. In the first days of our journey, Alfredo and I ate at nicer restaurants and stayed in clean motels. Although our original budget rated meager by U.S. standards, it allowed us to eat well. With over half of our remaining money stolen and still having more stops on our trip back, the circumstances forced us into an economy plan.

One night, we ended up sleeping on kitchen tables at the church where we ministered. My back suffered for Jesus that night, but we survived and enjoyed spending time with so many interesting people and seeing new places.

Our frugal travel procedures often meant buying from street vendors. Merchants on every side pushed little vegetables and fruits in our direction, trying to make a quick sale. The food quality did not compare to restaurant food, but we rejoiced at these bargain alternatives. In the Cuzco markets, you never know for sure what you might be eating. It is a mystery meal, but usually delicious just the same. I learned an important lesson: secure my money.

*Sanhedrin*
After being away from Lima for two weeks, Alfredo and I arrived just in time for the big Sunday night church service, which capped off each weekend. After eight months in Peru, my time grew short before I would return to the United States and my uncertain future. By this point, I found myself totally smitten with Emma, even though our time spent together happened only in groups. Other single men in our thousand-member church must have shared my appreciation for her. This thought worried me.

The Bible school's strict dating rules continued to cramp my style and thwart my plans. Like the other students, Emma signed up to rules that put her focus on her studies and strengthening her relationship with God. The three-year curriculum proved intensive with no time for finding a future spouse. Those in charge of the school hoped students would fall in love with Jesus, not each other. Romance did not have a place on their agenda.

The circumstances became more torturous as my love grew.

In May 1986, as my time grew short, Emma still had two years left in her studies. She loved Peru and chose Bible school in Lima instead of joining her parents for college in the United States. Her heart remained with the Peruvian people and with the inner-city church in Lima. This character trait that threatened my opportunity to win her heart made me love and respect her all the more. She chose busy fourteen-hour days in Lima over a softer, more comfortable life in the U.S.

Emma's ancestors came as slaves from Africa to Peru. Two of her grandparents, born and raised in Pisco, moved to Lima to find a better life. Emma's mother accepted Christ and started a new spiritual heritage for the family.

My biggest rivals for Emma's love would come from her Bible school classmates. As soon as she graduated, a plethora of suitors lay in wait to ask Emma's hand in marriage. She opened as a blossoming flower, maturing in body and spirit.

Growing agitated over my impending departure, I could no longer contain my burgeoning love. I wrote Emma a letter right before leaving for Cuzco. The words, painstakingly crafted, described what a special place she had won in my being. I explained my strong ambition to win her heart. With no direct contact at the Sunday night services, I sent my love letter through one of the pastor's wives. Then, I left for Cuzco the next day. For the two weeks of my trip, I impatiently worried over the contents of her reply. Maybe the response of my dreams waited for me at the Barriger's when I returned. Could it be?

Sitting in church upon my return, I stared like a sick puppy in her direction. If only I could catch her eye, she might give me a hint about her response. The church proceedings followed their normal format, but the time dragged by at the slowest of paces. Maybe I would get my answer soon after the final amen. Oh Lord, let the answer be yes and amen!

Following the last song, Pastor Estrada located me and

asked to have a word. While I agreed, I hoped he would make it quick. Emma might be standing outside talking with friends. Perhaps we could have a word before she headed to her dorm. My heart kept beating faster with anticipation.

Despite my distraction, the pastor led me into the midst of a group of very serious-looking men: pastors and leaders of the Lima church. I called many of them friends and a few, even mentors. Smiling like an innocent sheep, I wondered why none returned my pleasant expression.

"We need to talk to you," Pastor Estrada began. "Over these past months, we have grown to know you and love you very much. We took you into our fellowship and trusted you. But you have broken our rules by sending an inappropriate letter to Emma. This is a serious matter."

All the blood drained out of my face, and I thought I might fall over. This group of angry-looking men reminded me of the biblical Sanhedrin. They had judged my conduct wanting and next would be the sentencing. No words came out of my mouth, just a deer-in-the-headlights stare. Did they believe in stoning?

"I want to talk to you in my office tomorrow morning at 9:00 a.m."

I trembled at his words. "Yes, Pastor Estrada, I will meet you then."

Later, I learned that Emma, not wanting to get into any trouble herself, showed my letter to a leader of the Bible school. This led to the impending doom of my meeting with Pastor Estrada. I lay awake for hours that night. Believing their judgment unfair, I worried about the future.

Even though it meant big trouble with my hosts, I did not regret sending the letter and making my feelings known. What choice did I have? Time ebbed away, and soon I would be far from Lima. My love for Emma held urgency because the opportunity appeared fleeting. Would she even remember me two years from now?

Robert, my host, thought my predicament the funniest thing he'd ever seen or heard. He knew how infatuated I'd become with Emma and how seriously the pastors regarded the school's rules and mores. Robert and his wife probably viewed my love as simple infatuation, blown out of proportion by myself and the holy fathers. To my surfer host, my situation appeared to be much ado about nothing.

**********************************

The next morning, I arrived on time at Pastor Estrada's office. If I had a tail, it would have been between my legs.

Pastor Estrada began his speech. "Okay David, you are leaving us in two weeks. Who knows if you will ever return to Peru?" His tone sounded heavy, and his face looked severe. I shifted in my seat. "We understand your affection, but this letter-sending is not proper. It is a breach of our trust. Do you understand?"

"Yes sir," I said. Sweat broke out on my forehead.

He continued. "Despite our feelings regarding the seriousness of your behavior, we have come up with a way you can explore your relationship with Emma."

I couldn't help squirming in my seat. My stomach churned into knots while he spoke. "Yes, Pastor," I offered weakly.

"This is how you can get to know Emma better while showing proper respect for our rules. Once you leave Peru, you may write to Emma once every three months. Until she completes the Bible school curriculum, do not contact her more often than quarterly. Understand, you are to write to her only as a friend writes to another friend, and nothing more. We reserve the right to read your letters before we give them to Emma."

I felt so in love with Emma by this point that no procedure

could deter me. My plan amounted to going along with whatever Pastor Estrada demanded.

"Sounds fair to me," I said, slumping back in my seat with relief.

In the two weeks before heading back to the States, one mission lay before me: to get to know Emma better. Even though we could speak only as friends, I needed to let her know the truth. I absolutely loved her more than any person had ever loved another.

Before leaving Lima, we took a few walks when she had free time, but always with an escort. These final moments together became a sweet ending to my time with the Barrigers. Because of the letter and the hoopla surrounding it, Emma got the message. She understood the depths of my feelings for her. Her mind and heart stayed on serving the Lord, but she opened the door to knowing me better. She may have been far from convinced that she might someday hitch her star to my wagon, but I at least had a chance.

After I left Peru, we didn't know that it would be twenty months before I would see Emma again. We stayed obedient to and diligent in following the Bible school's rules. Every three months, she and I exchanged letters. Then, the mail from her suddenly stopped.

# 4

# Learning Costa Rica and Invading Cuba

Having developed an appetite for missions in Peru, my zeal only grew through the coming months. After prayer and months back in the United States, I decided my next step of preparation would include a language school in Costa Rica. After being there a short time, it was time for a scheduled letter to Emma. Although she had my new address, no letter came in return. Perhaps something happened with the mail between Lima and San Jose. While I trusted our budding affection for each other, the silence weighed on me.

At the six-month point, another letter flowed easily from my hand. Then, the torture began. Each day the walk to the post office seemed longer. The postmaster grew tired of seeing me. When he saw me walk through the door, without a word from me, he would look in my direction and say, "No letter today."

I resigned myself to the idea that Emma had forgotten me. What if another Bible-toting young hombre won her heart? Perhaps life alone in a monastery awaited me. Not being Catholic, the monk idea wouldn't work.

One day, I trekked to the post office holding my usual personal pity party with each step. My one best love had forgotten me. Still, my affections remained faithful. If there had been a tin can on that street, I would have been kicking the can along as I walked. What if one of my Peruvian friends had stolen her heart? What if I never learned how or why it happened? What makes people fall in love anyway?

"It's me again, Mr. Postmaster," I said. my face pointed at the floor.

"Hola, David," he said in return, much brighter than usual.

"I know, I know—no mail for me again."

"Not so fast. I don't have one letter for you today." He smiled. "Believe it or not, I have two letters for you."

Imagine my joy when I saw that both letters sported Emma's familiar penmanship, one postmarked three months earlier and another from six months in the past. I left the post office singing "Oh Happy Day." As soon as I could be alone, I poured over the letters and drank in every word. Like rain on parched earth, her words fed my heart and soul. Life transformed from hideous to glorious in one afternoon. Our date with destiny still might be on, and everything again grew right with my life.

Costa Rica overwhelmed me with its luscious green landscapes. In downtown San Jose, majestic trees flank wide boulevards, and Spanish architecture rose grandly above well-kept lawns. The masonry and red-tiled roofs lend a

# Learning Costa Rica and Invading Cuba

sophisticated air to the place.

The language school gave new meaning to the term immersive study. With five hours of classes and tons of homework each day, I learned so much in a short time. While the curriculum churned at a blistering pace, the fellowship and Christian atmosphere made up for the sacrifices. I stayed with a Costa Rican family and spoke Spanish with them.

"David, your Spanish improves daily," my host said.

"All this because I know the phrase for taking out the garbage?" I asked.

"I am impressed by your command of garbage," he said, smiling. "You are learning at a much faster rate than other students we have hosted."

On the weekends, I worked in a small orphanage on the outskirts of town. The fifteen or twenty kids ranged in age from one to eleven years. While not called to work with children, I loved those little ones with every ounce of my being.

From time to time while serving there, one or another of the younger kids would be adopted. All of us on staff rejoiced with those who were adopted, but grieved for those left behind. How it hurt my soul to see the pain on the faces of the older children. Over time, they realized that as they aged, they became less desirable for a family to adopt them. It made me love all orphaned children even more.

My time at the Spanish school in Costa Rica came to a close. Most of my Costa Rica classmates had gone to Bible school before going to language school. That meant many of them headed off to their permanent mission field assignments. Never one to do things like everyone else, I put off Bible school until I had more Spanish-language training. I figured that doing Bible school in English could set back my assimilation into Spanish culture and cause me to forget my Spanish. In prayer, the Lord led me to a Bible school in Quito, Ecuador. Perfect, Bible school, taught in Spanish, and closer to Emma.

The fellowship of my fellow students sustained me during this period, and I loved many of them like brothers. Although my new language skills and memories would come with me, it broke my heart to leave behind "my kids" from the orphanage. With tears, I hugged them each good-bye on my last day. With a hasta luego, I choked up leaving the parking lot, hoping someday I might see them again. Deep in my heart, I knew I probably never would. This would be one of those times to entrust the future of these precious children to God. While I would have loved to adopt each one, I knew God had other things planned for me.

*Quito, Ecuador*
The time arrived for the next phase of my missionary education, so off to Ecuador I went to study with an amazing ministry called Cristo al Mundo or Christ to the World. Quito is a gorgeous city in the high northern Andes Mountains, not too far from the border with Colombia.

The men's dormitory was an option. However, being around men day and night for the past year, other options appealed to me. God provided a house, located halfway up the volcano and downwind of the Quito airport. Living by myself gave me more time alone with God and less time smelling dirty men's socks. It seemed ideal.

I loved getting up early each morning to pray. Watching out my window, my view looked into the cabins of giant Boeing 747s as they approached the Quito airport. It served as a unique vantage point for prayer. After being in my rental house for only a week, Jorge Gonzalez, the director of the school, asked to see me. He impressed me from the start, looking professional and comporting himself with dignity. His salt-and-pepper hair lent a distinguished flourish to his neat clothing. His speech sounded like I imagined a full professor at an Ivy League school might speak.

## Learning Costa Rica and Invading Cuba

"Mr. Gonzalez, did you want to see me?" I asked, hiking up my pants.

"David, come in and sit with me. How is everything going so far?"

"Just fine. Great group of students, faculty, and I am learning so much already."

"Good. Good. Time is short. Let me get to the point. I have an opportunity for you. How would you like to become the director of the men's dorm?"

My first thought escaped my lips: "What an honor. Wow! Great! How can I say no? I would like to help." Even as the words floated in the air, something told me I hadn't thought things through, much less prayed to ask God's opinion.

"Great to hear," Mr. Gonzalez said. "I am impressed with your manner and the way you interact with other students. I've heard great things from two of your instructors. Now, just for your information, I must leave the country next week. That explains the urgency of filling this position. Jose will brief you on the responsibilities. Let me know if you have questions before I go."

"How long is your planned trip?" I asked, sensing this information might be critically important.

"Two months, give or take, but the faculty has everything under control. Don't worry. You will just need to look after the men in the dorm."

I left the meeting pleased that he thought enough of me to offer this responsibility. Other thoughts crept in later that evening. First, I had grown accustomed to my solo lifestyle in the house on the hill. With the intense course workload, how would I balance time to grow in my relationship with God and look after the men?

Little did I know at the outset the challenging mess that faced me. We had fifteen Ecuadorians and fifteen Colombians living in the dorm. Several of the Colombians had accepted the Lord while in prison and had just gotten out of jail. Many of them had never worked a day in their lives at legitimate employment. You might say several of the men had responsibility issues. Others came from a tough-as-nails upbringing and needed help adapting to polite society.

Having two bordering nationalities under one roof can be a challenge. In Central and South America, national pride and rivalry run deep. Colombians and Ecuadorans are famous for not getting along with each other. Although there may be no east and west in Christ, there is definitely north and south for Colombian and Ecuadoran brothers.

As the term progressed, I discovered what a hornet's nest surrounded me. Although the men professed faith in Jesus, let's say God and I had a few rough edges to smooth out. Only by God's grace, I came out alive, with ten fingers and ten toes attached. The Lord heard my frequent cries for help with leadership and wisdom. On the other side, the dorm director job sped up my spiritual growth. The responsibilities, including sorting out conflict, brought me much closer to God.

Although he set me up for a difficult assignment, Jorge Gonzalez and I remain great friends to this day. However, I still believe he owes me a steak dinner or two.

*Cuba*

While in Quito, we heard much about Cuba. Christians in the island nation faced harsh conditions and lacked many essentials. Alexander Moreno, a Cuban refugee to Ecuador, shared details of the plight of his church mates in Cuba, their struggles and pain.

Alexander and I became fast friends. I drank in his interesting stories and spiritual insights. His description of Cuban believers with no Bibles touched me. His tales of strong revival in the face of persecution energized me. The

Communist government of Cuba feared the Christian church. As Alexander described, the adamant atheists of the Castro regime did everything possible to put a lid on the gospel. Neighborhood moles would curry favor with the government by informing on Christians.

He explained how these informers spied on suspected Christians. The few people who owned Bibles kept them hidden, never showing them in public. The penalty for distributing Bibles on the island amounted to ten years in prison. As long as the Christians did not proselytize or try to spread the gospel, the spies just watched from the sidelines. But if a Christian shared his faith, he (or she) might disappear. Far from trusting the police, many Cuban Christians assumed the police took their missing loved ones. The prospect of losing a family member in this way struck a chord with me. My empathy meter climbed off the charts.

The picture of Cuban brothers and sisters needing Bibles burned in my mind and heart. A friend and I from Bible school decided to make a clandestine trip into Cuba. While U.S. law forbade Americans even to travel to the island nation, my desire to spread the good news about Jesus overcame my instinct for self-preservation. Blame it on the impetuousness of youth. We made our plans with help from Alexander.

The two of us packed several Bibles in a box, along with our clothes and supplies. Our naiveté showed in everything we packed. As soon as we got off the plane in Havana, my heart rate tripled. I mustered deep courage and managed to avoid wetting myself as we lined up for customs inspection.

Officials checked and pawed through everything we'd brought. My prayers hit a high pitch when I approached the front of the line.

"What's in this box?" asked a soldier in an olive-drab uniform. His dark, penetrating stare unnerved me. His large, hairy fingers tapped on the top of the cardboard container.

"Just books we need to study during our trip," I said. Our pretense for coming to Cuba included research for our studies. Back in Quito, our cover story as students sounded convincing. We *are* students, right? Now, our story petered out minutes after landing in Havana. Lying never had been my strong suit.

The customs police confiscated the Bibles faster than ice cream melts in the Havana sun. Chances are the Scriptures were sold on the Cuban black market. While the profits, no doubt, ended up in the hands of greedy government officials, we trust the Bibles found their way to the right people.

"Cassette tapes?" the soldier asked. By now, he looked like a hunter who stumbled on a pond full of geese.

Confiscation of the Bibles did not deter me from continuing with my pretense. "We are on break from school in Ecuador," I said, trying to look cheerful. "We must have the tapes to study while visiting here. I have a final exam when I get back."

The guard looked bored by this point and let us through with the teaching tapes. With God's help, our Christian hosts duplicated the tapes and distributed them to churches throughout Cuba.

We also brought extra clothing and money for the churches we planned to visit. Several pieces of clothing got confiscated, but most made it past security. One hilarious note, the guards' suspicions spiked when they found one clothing item. They wondered why two grown men brought a young girl's dress to Cuba for our vacation. Later we realized what rank amateurs we were at smuggling.

While some of our cargo got confiscated, we made it through with the money, a few Bibles, and several teaching tapes.

Although 1988, our trip felt like stepping back in time to the year 1959 when Fidel Castro took over the island nation. As we rode from the airport, the sights and sounds mesmerized us. The old cars looked majestic as they moved rhythmically around Havana. Most of the buildings stood unrenovated since the 1950s. The exceptions to the decay included government buildings, which looked grand and in good repair. Obviously, the government had the money and the power in Cuba. As the book Animal Farm portrays totalitarian society, everyone may be equal, but some are more equal than others.

To call the weather very warm is a gross understatement. In the car, we kept the windows lowered, trying to capture a cool breeze now and then. One side benefit to natural air conditioning: we got an immediate immersion into Cuban culture. The liveliest and most intoxicating Latin music blared from speakers everywhere we went. The smells of spicy chicken and sea breezes filled the air. Cubans treated us well and acted friendly toward us. Their happiness encouraged my soul and somewhat reshaped my life view. How can I sweat small details when I've seen such perseverance of the human spirit?

"David, you and your friend must be very careful out on the streets," said one of the church people we met in Havana. "You can get into serious trouble. We don't want that for you."

"I understand, but God is watching over us," I replied. "He will protect us."

"Learn this Russian phrase, nyet de le Ya ne ponimayu. It means I don't understand you."

They wanted us to pretend we were Russian. In those days in Cuba, nobody wanted contact with visiting Russians. Getting on the wrong side of Russian overlords could be a quick way to seal your own death warrant. If people believed we came from Russia, they would leave us alone.

The pace of life in Cuba registered much slower than anywhere else I had lived, even the Shenandoah Valley. Most Cubans had no money and little to do. Too few jobs for too many people equaled massive idleness. We were disconcerted at seeing so many men just sitting around. I later pondered how much talent must have been wasted. People pay a big price when their government gets off track.

Pastor Alejandro hosted our visit to Havana. He treated us quite well and answered our hundreds of questions patiently. We wanted to learn everything Cuban to better understand our Christian brothers and sisters living there.

"Why are those people standing in line?" I asked as we drove by a storefront.

"That store must be selling something special today, maybe meat," Pastor Alejandro said. "Many times, the store shelves are empty. Word travels fast when new inventory arrives."

"Wow. You don't have enough food here." The realization sounded lame coming out of my mouth, but the words hit me hard. I did not mean to sound condescending, but it became an aha moment for me. People trapped on an island with limited natural resources faced extreme hardship. I wished I could change things for them.

"We get by with help from each other," he said. Another simple statement, his words became the theme of our visit. The Cuban culture included a closeness seldom seen elsewhere.

The next morning, Pastor Alejandro drove us into the countryside. We began many days of visiting house churches and other underground meetings. We enjoyed fellowship and offered encouragement to the wonderful Christians we met. Their faith brightened our lives beyond what we could have imagined. They appreciated our risky visit to their country.

The fellowship in those church meetings differed from other places I'd been, even the poorest villages in Peru. Despite persecution and the threat of imminent imprisonment, their deep hunger for God and His Word showed on the countenances of the people. Every church and meeting place we visited would be jam-packed with earnest seekers of the gospel. They stood at the doors and outside the windows, straining to hear even a part of what any of us said. Services began at 9:00 p.m. and often lasted until 1:00 a.m.

Cuban Christians enraptured us with excitement for the gospel and their fervor for the faith. Organizers of the meetings would try to keep the noise levels low, so unbelieving neighbors would not discover them. Complaints to the authorities might permanently shutter the meetings. Sometimes, worshipers just could not contain themselves. They robustly praised the Lord and sang hymns with unfettered jubilation.

After a typical service, our church hosts gave Pastor Alejandro, my partner, and me a plate of their best food. We hungrily devoured whatever they put before us and thanked God for it. Late into the night, we tried to make ourselves comfortable, spending the night at the church. We brought along primitive bedrolls that the underground church in Havana provided for our journey. The constant travel wiped us out by the end of those nights; we could have slept on concrete. A few times, we indeed slept on very hard surfaces. Fortunately, I brought along a young man's body during this trip, and my back rapidly recovered.

Often, the same people who worshiped until 1:00 a.m. woke us up with their fervent prayers at five in the morning. We could hear them in adjoining rooms, praying and seeking God. The night meeting had ended only a few hours earlier, but these people, hungering for more, returned to the meeting place.

Youth aside, the extreme heat and humidity sapped our strength. Rustic and uncomfortable, the daily challenges contributed to our fatigue. We had no alternative but to drink the local water and pray against any damaging side effects. Cubans proved so gracious, in many ways showing us their best hospitality.

"Here's a fan," one man said in Spanish. "It will stir a little breeze for you. Eduard will return it to me tomorrow."

I thanked him profusely for loaning us a prized possession. The fan not only kept us cooler, but it also helped keep the super-sized Cuban mosquitoes at bay. Our bodies were worn out, but our spirits rose as the trip continued.

When our time in a village ended, we usually traveled under cover of darkness to the next church in a neighboring town. In our twelve days of travel, we visited eighteen different churches. God showed great mercy to us while we toured the island nation. At no point did the police stop us or question any of our activities. No Cubans got into trouble with authorities because of our visit. Our main gift may have been the encouragement that Christians elsewhere in the world loved Cubans and prayed for them.

One night, Pastor Alejandro noticed the brakes going out on his car. Since he often acted the joker, we did not believe him at first.

"Is this one of your crazy jokes?" I asked.

"David, I promise you I am not joking," Pastor Alejandro replied. "Look at my foot."

In the dim lighting, I could see his foot push the brake all the way to the floorboard. The car did not respond. We rumbled along with no way to stop. The roads were almost empty, so Alejandro nursed the car along to the next village. When we eased up to his friend's house, Pastor Alejandro knocked on the door until his mechanic buddy got out of bed to look at the brakes.

The extended action of knocking on the rough-looking wooden door reminded me of a Bible story. In Luke, Jesus talks of a man trying to get his neighbor out of bed to borrow food. The neighbor says no because he and his family are in bed for the night. "I say to you, though he (the neighbor) will not rise and give to him because he is his friend, yet because of his persistence he will rise and give him as many as he needs" (Luke 11:8).

The mechanic turned on a single, bare light bulb and set up his little bench near the car. The scene looked surreal. Here we were, sitting in Cuba with a broken-down car, watching a man in a white t-shirt repair our brakes under a light bulb.

Alejandro's friend figured out that a gasket had blown in the master cylinder which controls the brakes. As I looked around that sleepy village, I silently wondered where our mechanic would find an auto parts store open at 2:00 a.m. With Cuban ingenuity, he wouldn't need a store.

The mechanic pulled out a large, thick piece of rubber from an old tractor tire. With his machete, he hacked off a small piece. Then, using an ingenious machine he had rigged up, he turned the piece of rubber into a gasket just the right size. He reassembled the rebuilt master cylinder, and we were on our way. The creativity of the Cuban people inspired me. With little, they did much. Mechanics must have been miracle workers to keep those gorgeous old cars running. They had no option but to fabricate replacement parts on the island.

One particular worship service still sticks in my mind. It began with the music of a 1950s organ, played at a low volume. While the youth led several worship songs, faith-filled faces shone as they brightly sang under a dim light. My buddy from Bible school preached his heart out. Though not a deep spiritual message, his words rang full of hope. Those brave enough to attend drank in every word, rapt in their attention. Just a few worshipers brought their Bibles. Those who did grasped these prized possessions tightly, cherishing the Word of God. It warmed my heart to witness their love for God's Word.

Throughout our trip we never saw a Bible lying around on the floor or unattended. Even though these dear ones loved their Bibles, they would sometimes cut the bindings to share portions of Scripture with those who had none.

We found every service packed with fervent believers. Their passion lit our hearts on fire. Despite the best efforts of the repressive regime, an amazing revival burned hot across Cuba.

One of the most bizarre miracles I saw up to that point in my life still amazes me. People showed us their teeth. With little access to dentistry, most people had no money and had never seen a dentist. Teeth problems can fester if not treated.

In answer to their fervent prayers, God saw their need and miraculously fixed problems in their mouths. Many people showed us gold-looking fillings, which they said had simply appeared in their mouths. They claimed the fillings had fixed years-old dental decay. While I have no explanation or biblical basis, I know what I saw and what they said. They had a need, and God sovereignly met it. With my own eyes, I have seen gold-like fillings in the mouths of Cuban Christians. There is no way they could afford gold or any other type of fillings. I can't explain it, but I saw it.

*Havana*

While my friend and I traveled around the island with Alejandro, back in Havana, Pastor Hector duplicated the teaching tapes we brought. When we returned to Havana, he showed us the secret room in his house where the duplicating machines and blank tapes stayed hidden. We felt so honored to see this secret place where the gospel message emanated to many of the island's Christians. We left our teaching tapes in his care, happy to know they might be a blessing for years to come.

On one of our last nights in Havana, Pastor Alejandro took us downtown. "Let's go to our most famous ice cream store," he said. "We will take a taxi."

In those days, Soviet-made motorized tricycles passed as cabs in Cuba. As we breezed through the streets, the heat and smells of Havana filled the air. At one point, our taxi slowed, and I rubbed my eyes in disbelief. I saw a team of mules pulling a MiG fighter jet with its wings folded back. Unsure what to make of the sight, I pulled out my camera.

"No!" my companions whispered forcefully.

"You could disappear in prison for taking that picture," Pastor Alejandro cautioned.

I will never forget the sight of that jet plane being pulled by mules, like two centuries colliding. Neither will I forget the shudder that rattled through me as I contemplated disappearing forever in a Cuban prison.

The ice cream at Helados Copelia cooled our bodies, brightened our mood, and filled our stomachs. It tasted so rich and creamy with bright strawberry flavor. My palate found it amazing. Interestingly enough, they served the ice cream on metal plates. In the whole time I visited this mysterious island, I never saw a disposable plate or cup. They charged us little for our lovely ice cream treats, but the taste registered more luxurious than any ice cream I have ever eaten.

As we prepared to leave, the Christians we'd met in Havana grew emotional ... and so did I.

"We will miss you so much," Pastor Alejandro said. "You have energized us with your visit and met many needs. May God watch over you and keep you safe."

Tears poured from my eyes. Parting from these brave souls left me thankful for my faith in God's protection for them. We became old friends in just under two weeks. Their sacrifices for the gospel warmed and encouraged my heart. We prepared to leave, strengthened in our resolve to accept whatever assignment God had for us on the mission field.

Their daily courage and brotherly love neutralized my fear. I thrived on seeing God's power in the face of a government trying so hard to eradicate Christianity. These followers of Jesus gave us their best food and the best accommodations they could spare. They won a permanent place in our hearts.

Conventional wisdom among missionaries includes bragging on the food of each culture where we serve. I tried this with my Havana friends. "What region of Cuba has the best food?"

"Miami," my hosts said in unison, laughing. "That's where you'll find the best ingredients! Thanks to communism, we only get second-rate groceries here." Although this sounded right, my Cuban friends' sense of humor added to my admiration for them.

Although illegal for us to be there, the Cuban government admitted me on my U.S. passport. More important, they let me leave. Once back in Ecuador, I took a pocket knife to the Cuban seal on my passport. I didn't want to return to the U.S. with documentation proving I had committed a crime by going to Cuba.

Years later, it saddened me to hear Pastor Alejandro had passed to heaven after a bout with cancer. He will always have such a special place in my personal Christian Hall of Fame, while Cuba and its lovely people retain a unique place in my heart. I can see why Ernest Hemingway liked the island so much. Cubans are amazing people.

# 5

## Proposing and Wedding the Peruvian Way

In January 1988, I returned to Lima to reconnect in person with Emma. My love for her had grown by leaps and bounds since leaving the country twenty months earlier. With her impending graduation from Bible college, I knew I must get engaged and seal the deal for the marriage of my dreams. Not wanting to run afoul of the Bible school authorities again, this time I confided my plan to Pastor Estrada.

"David, my spiritual son, it is so special to have you back with us for a visit," Pastor Estrada said. He studied me with those piercing eyes, softened only by his half-smile.

"I'm so thankful to see you again. I've learned many things

these past couple of years in Costa Rica and Ecuador. God is doing an amazing work in both places."

"Then, you are ready for full-time mission work. Is that your plan?" Estrada asked.

I did not want to avoid his question as much as change the subject to the real purpose of my visit. "You probably guessed why I am here. Emma and I have followed all the rules. We wrote each other on schedule. We love each other more each day. With her impending graduation, I plan to ask her to be my wife. I already have the ring picked out."

"Oh, I see." A troubled look crossed Pastor Estrada's face. Bubbly and effusive a few minutes before, now he looked like a man who just lost his best friend.

"Well, we will come back for visits," I said, trying to provide some form of comfort. With no aversion to returning to Peru, even permanently someday perhaps, that moment seemed like the right time to open a new chapter. After completing my training and waiting for Emma to do the same, we longed for a fresh start somewhere else. As a practical matter, my support network barely paid enough for me to go to Bible school. How would it fund two people hoping to begin a family?

"So, you plan to take this beautiful jewel away from us? We have invested so much time and energy into Emma's training to serve God."

He stumped me with that statement. Pastor Estrada's piercing stare revealed a side of him seldom seen. I did not see the question coming. Not knowing how to respond, I stared down at my shoes. Not fancy shoes or new shoes, but the loafers held my attention—much safer than looking at my former mentor. The loafers psychologically comforted me but disclosed no answers. The silence hung in the air a while.

Pastor Estrada finally spoke again, "Well, tell me how she responds. We love both of you very much. I want the best for you."

"Thank you," I said, rising to leave before he put me in emotional handcuffs.

Once away from the office, I invited Emma out for our first real date. We would be alone together at a restaurant, like grown-up adults. She accepted. Suddenly, nervousness welled up. It is funny in life how a few key moments seem to shape our destiny. Despite all that I knew about her by that time, it felt impossible to predict how she might respond to a marriage proposal. Would she be willing to follow me to the ends of the earth, or at least to the U.S. while I regrouped?

Nervously, we traveled together by bus to a quaint, neighborhood restaurant. With the atmosphere perfectly Peruvian, I slipped down on one knee.

"Emma, you know why I came back to Lima. Would you marry me?" I withdrew the ring from the box.

She smiled the most angelic smile. "Yes, David Bredeman, I will marry you."

The weight of a thousand dinosaurs lifted from my chest. I jumped up and kissed her right there in front of God and everyone. The girl who dominated my dreams stepped permanently into my reality. Our engagement began.

Our friendly waiter witnessed what happened from a few feet away. He rushed over to congratulate us. "This is so exciting," he said in Spanish. "Let me take a picture for you." He picked up my camera and snapped a photograph we still treasure. Emma showed off her ring finger with the symbol of my love sitting on it. After a long, difficult conquest, she would at last be mine.

Secretly and without my permission, another pastor prebriefed Emma that I planned to propose. When I heard about it days later, furious doesn't describe my tirade. How could anyone spoil the surprise of a marriage proposal? Whatever his motives, the night of our engagement remained magical for me. In the end, she agreed to spend the rest of her life with me, and that is truly all that mattered.

*The Wedding*
By early 1989, my long-distance relationship with Emma would finally transition to happily ever after. After graduating from Bible school in Ecuador and proposing marriage, I returned to the U.S. to work and to save money for our wedding. Time seemed to drag. The main thing that occupied my mind: getting back to Peru and hugging my betrothed one. Although expensive, our talks over the phone solidified my love all the more.

Finally, the day arrived for me to fly to Peru and begin final preparations for our marriage in the church where the Lord had trained me in ministry, Catedral de Fe. This house of God became the nest where I found Emma and learned to adore missions. The whole experience prepared me for a remarkable life and solidified Peru's special rank in my heart.

When talking with Pastor Estrada, he surprised me with a loosely veiled reference to an Old Testament story. "David, you owe me seven years of work," he said. Although I laughed off his comments, his words sunk into my brain and haunted my thoughts. When one of the biblical patriarchs, Jacob, wanted a certain woman for his bride, the young lady's father insisted that Jacob toil for him seven years to earn his blessing.

The Bible school faculty had put a lot of effort and time into training Emma and helping her grow in her faith. Pastor Estrada did not like me carting her off to the United States and both of us forgetting about the Peruvian people. I respected him, not just because he mentored me or because he planted three hundred churches. His love for me and for his flock radiated everywhere. A warm, but towering spiritual figure, he held much influence in the country and even today, he remains beloved by many. If we stayed near him, he could better shepherd our marriage and lives ahead.

His desire to keep us in Lima grew to an uncomfortable level. As we prepared for the wedding, he turned up the heat. "You are taking a gem from our church," he repeated one day. I smiled and tried to laugh it off.

Until we escaped Peru following the ceremony, it crossed my mind that some police or government official might try to hold us in the country against our will. In retrospect, this probably showed paranoia on my part. Pastor Estrada's stares and comments kept me nervous.

My mother, brother, and sister helped make our wedding day special by flying in from the U.S., as did Emma's parents. My brother served as my best man, the natural choice. I love and respect him very much.

While the ushers walked our mothers to their seats, my brother, sister and I would come down the petal-strewn middle aisle together and sit near the front. Over a thousand well-wishers crowded the church for this "family" wedding. Emma and I welled up with excitement, so honored and loved by this church we called home.

Like most grooms, my nerves bubbled hotter as the hour for the ceremony grew close. That's when the trouble started. I have an alter ego. His name is Loco Gringo, and I must keep him in check to avoid catastrophes. On this day of all days, the last thing any of us needed would be an embarrassing goof up.

As I stood near the back of the sanctuary, the scene looked magical with large candles mounted on poles at the end of every third row. Beautiful, clear glass globes surrounded candles and cast warm, yellowish light in all directions. I watched ten young girls parade up the main aisle, spreading fragrant flower petals along the way. Organ music played solemnly in the background. Everything began exactly according to plan— traditional, stately, and full of love.

Finally, it came time for my sister, brother and me to walk to the front of the sanctuary. With so many friends on either side of the church smiling and waving, I grinned almost uncontrollably. We glided up the aisle to the front row. That's when I caused a mini-disaster.

As we reached our places, only two chairs sat in the front row for the three of us—not the way we rehearsed. This wouldn't work, but there appeared an easy fix. Wanting so badly to make my sister feel comfortable and included, we needed a third chair. I glanced around and quickly spotted one in the next row.

Instead of having my sister slip back just one row, I thought it better to pull the additional seat into place. As I slid it forward, the chair closest bumped the towering candle stand. The globe and candle at the top teetered precariously. Before I fully comprehended the situation, hundreds of gasps emanated from the massive, wary congregation. Time seemed to hang in the balance for several seconds. Then, the whole apparatus plummeted to the floor in slow motion. With a mighty crash and then a resounding clanking sound, the glass exploded into a million pieces followed by the lamp stand bouncing along the tile floor. Candle wax spewed everywhere. Deathly silence fell over the assembly. With that, I made my indelible mark on Catedral de Fe.

An array of thoughts danced through my mind. Most of them included the phrase loco gringo. Loco gringo spoils wedding by knocking over candle stand. We can dress loco gringo up, but we can't take him anywhere. Loco gringo breaks centuries-old candle globe, resulting in seven years of bad luck. You get the idea.

Despite my miscue, the sacred service continued. Emma floated effortlessly down the aisle, her dress looked exquisite, her face completely obscured by an elaborate veil. She appeared not to notice the considerable wax splashed across the center aisle. The candle/globe disaster quickly faded from memory.

The church had numerous matrimonial traditions, and we partook in all of them. The ceremony itself took about two-and-a-half hours, longer than most basketball games.

Loco gringo saved one more goof-up for the vows. Following the plan, I translated the key parts of the ceremony for my English-speaking friends and relatives. We hoped this would help them follow along and survive the lengthy ceremony.

Although I felt proficient with my Spanish, I made one glaring error. I should have said, "I take Emma as my legitimate wife." Unfortunately, I substituted the term illegitimate where legitimate belonged. More giggling and murmuring from the mostly Spanish-speaking crowd. Glad that loco gringo has further amused you, I thought.

When the ceremony ended, Emma and I reversed our course up the center aisle, now married and loving it. The service concluded, and we enjoyed the cake and punch reception in the Cathedral de Fe social hall. With the large number of people that attend weddings at that church, no one expected a big meal or lavish after-party. All the same, we enjoyed one of the happiest days of our lives and further solidified my love for Emma and for Peru.

Once Emma and I married, there remained immigration hoops to jump through, including securing Emma's visa to come to the U.S. Throughout this process, I worried that Pastor Estrada just might be serious about that seven years of work. I finally breathed a sigh of relief once the plane door closed, and we took off for the U.S. In retrospect, how silly of me to think my former pastor and still-current friend would have hauled us off a plane and tried to force me to minister the gospel in Peru.

*Back in the USA*
Emma's parents and two of her three brothers lived in New Jersey. In our minds, we returned to the States to reconnect with our families and enjoy home life for a season.

Emma's mother, Maria, later told us that the first time she saw me, she intuited that I would become her daughter's husband. Although she believed the word to be from God, she did not immediately grow excited about the idea. Her lack of enthusiasm translated in her response to God. "That's between you and him, Lord. I will have nothing to do with it." Fortunately, she warmed up to me over the years. At least, I think so.

Married and back in the U.S., I thought we would spend six months at most before heading out to a new challenge on the mission field. I made no plans for where we might serve as missionaries, nor did I learn to build the required support network.

As life unfolded, our return to foreign missions took longer than either of us imagined. We first settled in Fairfax, Virginia. After being married just two months, Emma became pregnant. Christian Assembly Church, where I received my initial call to the mission field, became our church home. They rejoiced with us over our good news of a baby on the way. Once expecting a little one, the timing seemed off for jumping back out on a mission assignment.

After two years, our three-person family moved to my family's farm in the Shenandoah Valley. We attended Fishnet Christian Center. The church grew famous throughout Virginia and beyond for sponsoring a multi-day contemporary gospel music concert and camp-out. We helped, taught, and supported various aspects of ministry, while I earned a living cabinet-making.

Life continued happening, and we soon had child number two, and then a third. During all of this time, God remained patient with me. Deep in my heart, career satisfaction eluded me. Emma sensed the same thing. She and I put off major decisions, like buying a house, because we both intended to eventually return to missions. In the meantime, I kept working; she took care of the kids; and we ministered on weekends within the local church structure.

Small children changed my view of the mission field. My fatherly hormones bred protective feelings I'd never known. Working in a foreign country held risks and neither of us knew where we might go. In this way, my lack of faith overwhelmed reason. While yielding to God cedes control to Him, I realize His basic nature is good. We should have realized He would not place us in the middle of a war zone with three young kids.

In one of his epistles, the Apostle Paul summed up my situation: "Therefore we also pray always for you that our God would count you worthy of this calling and fulfill all the good pleasure of His goodness and the work of faith with power" (2 Thessalonians 1:11).

As the children got older, the Lord worked on me little by little. My stubborn streak resisted, but God is unrelenting. I threw myself into woodworking to support my family, perhaps hoping to drown out the voice that haunted me.

Sadly, my vision for missions faded into the background. Like so many other men and women with the call of God on their lives, I responded, "Later, Lord." Somewhere inside, I knew if I never went back to the mission field, I would not have considered my Christian life a complete success.

### Encounter with a Dump Truck

God used a giant fish to change Jonah's mind about ministry, but he used a truck accident to speak to Emma and me. One year after her birth, our youngest daughter Mary required surgery. Born with a dislocated hip, doctors wanted to wait until she turned one-year-old to operate. Once they fixed the hip, the doctor put her in a large cast. Emma had to keep the cast as clean as possible. Imagine working with a one-year-old post-surgery.

This time-consuming and laborious chore grew physically draining. The trip demanded vigilance with a child that age. Emma stayed exhausted from all the driving, even though I helped out with the other two children and tried to do my part.

One day, Emma yawned up a storm while navigating the usual forty-five minutes to pick up our son from school. She became drowsy and dozed off. Her car drifted left of center on a busy highway. Providentially, the driver of an oncoming dump truck saw her coming and blew his horn frantically. He tried valiantly to get off the road and avoid her car. The large vehicle had extra wheels along the side. Emma's car bounced off one of those wheels and ran off the pavement. When she came to, she found only one wheel and a bumper of her car had suffered damage. While this incident might have ended her life, the Lord intervened, preserving her. Abruptly, God used this near-miss to grab my attention.

As if waking from my long spiritual nap, the dump truck roused my interest in serving God again through missions. I humbled myself and asked, "What do you have in mind for me, Father?"

By that time, I started drinking wine in the evenings. It began slowly with a glass now and then. Eventually my imbibing progressed to a glass every day. I told Emma that I needed the wine for health reasons. In my heart, I recognized drinking alcohol could become a serious problem for me. Alcoholism haunted several members on my family tree. Up to that point, I had avoided it since becoming a committed Christian. Even with intentions of controlling myself, my wine consumption slowly increased until it reached two glasses each night.

As He is superb at doing, the Lord arranged events for maximum impact. First, Emma experienced her rendezvous with the dump trunk. Next, she and I planned to attend a special church conference back in Peru. We both grew excited to return, now ten years after our wedding. Emma's parents agreed to care for the kids while we traveled. Her mother and father drove down from New Jersey and stayed at our house. They intended to stay for two weeks. Wintertime in the northern hemisphere meant a nice respite in store for us in Lima, with much warmer temperatures.

Since I planned to drink no alcohol around our Peruvian church friends, I imbibed a little extra the night before our flight out. When the alarm rang on the morning of our departure, the window seemed to glow in an unusual way. I peered outside. God had dumped at least eight inches of fluffy snow on the Shenandoah Valley. The normal travel time to Dulles airport would have been ninety minutes in good conditions. Now, the bad weather might make us late. We needed to hurry to allow extra time before boarding our international flight.

After brushing off the car and quickly loading our suitcases into the trunk, we said our goodbyes and jumped in for the lengthy drive. Once behind the wheel, I realized my mind seemed groggy, and my head felt hung over, definitely not the right condition to begin a tricky drive and then a lengthy flight. With great effort, I maneuvered the car down our long, hilly driveway to the quiet, snow-covered road below. Although I slid a bit now and then, we somehow made it onto the highway.

"Be careful," Emma urged. "Just go very slow."

"Yes, dear," I replied through a worsening headache. "The driveway was slick, but I'm going as slow as possible. God will watch over us. Don't worry."

Still experiencing the after-effects of drinking hours earlier, I should not have been driving at all. Anyone would need all their faculties for the slick, treacherous roads. Before we made it very far down the country road, our car started sliding. I reacted wrongly, over-steering and slamming on my brakes, sending us into 360-degree spins.

Amid the spinning, I heard God say, "This is your life, David. You are out of control and there is nothing you can do to keep control."

After what seemed like an eternity, we stopped spinning and glided into the ditch with a resounding crunch. Emma and I sat motionless a few minutes while gathering our composure and silently praying. The engine purred in the background as large snowflakes swirled around us.

As a country boy, I could get out of a ditch without calling for help. In less than ten minutes, we found ourselves back on the snowy roadway.

"At least I missed all the mailboxes," I said, hoping to ease the tension.

Emma just folded her arms and glanced in my direction. We continued with white knuckles and wide-open eyes, eventually arriving safely at Dulles airport. God used the experience to begin a much-needed change in me.

This second close call shook me up and prompted me to remain quiet during our flights to Peru. All the noise in my head ceased. In the silence, I sensed impending doom unless I made major changes. The psalmist may have experienced something similar when he wrote, "Unless the Lord had been my help, my soul would soon have settled in silence" (Psalm 94:17).

### *A Key Visit to Peru*

As soon as the jetway to the terminal in Lima opened, we encountered stifling temperatures. Emma's former hometown

## Proposing and Wedding the Peruvian Way

lay in the grip of midsummer. We walked happily through the airport. Hearing Spanish spoken in every direction provided a warm welcome and reset our minds. In the faces of other passengers, we saw a familiarity and reconnection to some of the happiest days of our lives.

At the conference, each evening's sermon seemed aimed at me. After four or five evenings in a row with the Lord digging deeper into my soul, one specific guest speaker from the United States spoke straight to my heart. A young woman, the then-current Miss South Carolina, took the podium and told a story that transformed me. She told us the devil tries to feed us misinformation about our destiny, but it's a lie. We need to listen to God's voice about our future, forget all the enemy's lies, and act on what we know to be true.

I realized I had been listening to the wrong voice that told me "Just give up. You are an alcoholic, just like your dad and grandfather. They died young because of booze, and so will you." Not only had I listened, but I had believed that lying prophecy. I had taken the message in, internalizing that view of myself.

As the young woman's talk ended, I turned to Emma and said, "I have to tell you something important. Come to the altar with me."

She smiled a beautiful smile and squeezed my hand. Perhaps God prepared her heart, knowing our circumstances needed to change. My wife seemed ready for whatever came next. We made our way to the crowded altar, located an empty spot, and knelt together. Many others across the sanctuary prayed their own prayers of repentance and dedication. A mighty movement of God swept through Catedral de Fe.

"Emma, I need to confess something. I've been drinking wine every night, not just for health reasons. It's gotten a foothold in my life, and I admit it. My consumption has progressed to the place of excess. Please forgive me. Things have to change. We must get on with our mission in life."

We both cried. In this moment of confession, chains fell off. The Scripture penned by John exploded in front of us: "If we confess our sins, he is faithful and just to forgive us our sins, and to cleanse us from all unrighteousness" (1 John 1:9).

Although I had been very astute at keeping my secret, I realized that I had hurt both of us. At the same time, my vision for missions returned. It became a place of transforming power, a turning point for me. In retrospect, I wonder if the wine had a numbing effect on my spirituality. Perhaps I did not hear God's Spirit as well under the influence.

For me to receive this life-changing experience with the Lord, He had to pull me from my comfortable home environment. The conference in Peru did just what I needed. From here, I recognized that somehow everything would be different.

Emma and I began planning to move our family of five to Lima. At the remote 1880s farmhouse on a three-hundred-acre farm in Virginia, I had sheltered my children. Whatever the plan, it had to include incremental adaptation. Concerned about the abrupt change of moving, not just to a city, but to a Latin America metro area of nine million people, we wanted to soften the transition for them.

Soon after we returned from Peru, God opened a door at a Spanish-speaking church in Herndon, Virginia. Emma and I helped out with ministry and enjoyed the supportive environment. At Cristo Redentor, we eased our children into new-to-them Spanish culture. New friends their age helped widen their circle of reference. At home, we added more and more Spanish words to our conversations.

Mike Havlin, our pastor at Cristo Redentor, had been Emma's professor at Bible school in Lima. He invited us to work with him in Herndon as a bridge assignment. Our family sorely needed this opportunity and we appreciated the chance. God used our time there to great benefit in our lives. At that point, Mike and his wife had over fifteen years of mission experience between them. They provided practical advice and emotional support.

Once we moved closer to the Herndon church, not everyone in our family responded well to the change. Our nine-year-old son Joshua summed up his feelings in a terse statement: "I hate it here! There's nothing to do."

I thought for a minute, then gave him an inspired answer. "Son, within a few blocks here, there are at least a dozen nine-year-old boys who would say the same thing if they moved to our 300-acre farm in the country."

He got the point. His ability to acclimate improved from that moment.

We served at the Herndon church for a year and a half while gaining momentum to go onto the mission field. We lined up financial supporters and became part of a large mission organization that would help us in several ways. The Lord confirmed His call on our lives many times during this period. Sometimes He spoke to us through a Bible study lesson or through a message preached from the pulpit. Other times, He used our children to teach us needed lessons.

After about a year at the Herndon church, the Havelins headed out for a new mission in Nicaragua. This further inspired us to get on with our goal of returning to the mission field

During this period, Emma, the children, and I returned to Christian Assembly for a worship service. Their informal style remained the tradition at their meetings. Their practical Christianity inspired us and helped us mature. Over the years, I returned there many times to raise support or just recharge.

Mary, our youngest, seemed adept at hearing the Lord's voice. During the worship time, the leader asked if anyone in the congregation wanted to offer a word of encouragement or a spiritual song. I had such a word in my spirit but felt unsure if this was the right time to share it. Mary, then four years old, stood up on my lap and asked, "Daddy, aren't you going to speak?" This boost emboldened me to speak out the word God had whispered. Her exhortation turned out to be a harbinger of her gifting, which showed up often on Emma's and my life journey.

The house near Herndon proved a significant blessing for us. During the time we lived there, I renovated it and sold it for a profit to help with the expenses of moving to Peru. We also held "The Mother of All Yard Sales." We put almost everything we owned in our front yard and peddled it. Although Emma and I perceived intellectually what must happen, the experience took an emotional toll on all of us.

The children, young and innocent, expressed excitement about our new adventure, but they did not get the cost of moving to Peru until the day of the sale. Perhaps, neither did Emma and I. Watching our five- and six-year-old daughters carrying some of their teddy bears to the front lawn to be sold is one picture I will never get out of my mind. The memory of seeing their little hearts break as they said good-bye to precious toys remains one of the hardest experiences of my life.

When we thought we could not cry anymore, I still had to load our golden retriever into the car and give him away to a friend. Watching the rear view mirror and seeing my kids crying as we drove off, my emotions tore at my heart. God held me close that night as I thought about the Scripture verses from Mark when Jesus comforted His disciples: "Assuredly, I say to you, there is no one who has left house or brothers or sisters or father or mother or wife or children or lands, for My sake and the gospel's, who shall not receive a hundredfold now in this time—houses and brothers and sisters and mothers and children and lands, with persecutions—and in the age to come, eternal life" (Mark 10:29b-30).

We sold our home and worked full-time to raise funds. The whole family started itinerating, speaking in churches and small groups, telling people about our plans. This process helped in building up funds and making new partners for our work. Within a few months, we found ourselves on the mission field.

# 6

# Jumping into Peru

In October 2000, we could not believe our eyes as dear friends came to the airport to wish us well and send us off to Peru. After eighteen months of preparation and hard work, our emotions teetered between excitement and apprehension. We left Catedral de Fe as newlyweds and would return as a family of five. For me, it felt surreal to know all our earthly possessions now fit into our luggage. Could we adjust to a different way of life? Would our kids get on board for learning more Spanish? What kind of schooling could we arrange for them? Where would we live?

When a single man, I could go anywhere without much

hassle. As long as I had a Bible and a sleeping bag, it worked. Now others depended on me. The challenge drove me to a new level of intimacy with God. He taught me to trust Him for the small and great aspects of our lives.

Our first apartment in this phase of life consisted of a two-bedroom unit on the third floor of a home. At first, we had only our beds and two plastic chairs. Spartan is a mild description compared to what we left in the States. Because of the steep climb up the stairs, we bought just a few pieces of furniture. The children adjusted as well as they could. Having no refrigerator for two months, Emma shopped almost daily for our food.

One big milestone came with the purchase of a small refrigerator. All of us stared at the clock as it counted down to four o'clock. Right on time, the delivery guy arrived and carried the appliance up the stairs. As soon as he left, four-year-old Mary walked up to the appliance and hugged it. "Oh great, a refrigerator!" she said with deep satisfaction.

As soon as we hit the ground in Lima, we became very busy in ministry. Our friends the Barrigers now pastored a different church, one experiencing tremendous growth. Due to Emma and I feeling close with them, we decided to work in their church, Comino de Vida.

Opportunities to serve popped up in a variety of places. Every two to three weeks, I would journey to the other side of the Andes to speak at conferences or work with pastors in remote outposts. It felt invigorating to be back in the action. Traveling on long bus rides and having close contact with distant people groups energized my spirit and excited my mind.

Not all of my trips merged well with family life. Emma remained back in Lima, caring for the children and working at various Commode Vida ministries. When I took off for the other side of the country, she had to get the kids ready for school, see them off, and then hurry to her volunteer ministry job.

One day at our apartment, the telephone rang, and I rushed to answer it. After a conversation of several minutes, I hung up and found my bride in the other room.

"Emma, that was Pastor Peter Hocking on the phone. He invited me to share at a conference in the Northern Amazon."

Brushing her hair to one side with her hand, she looked up from her morning devotional book. "When is it?" she asked. Emma stayed calm in these situations.

"That's the only problem," I said. "The meetings fall on the same week as American Thanksgiving."

Emma responded with a loud "Hmm" but said nothing. I sort of knew what this meant. Although not in the United States any more, she and the kids still wanted to celebrate and enjoy the familiar holiday. By going away, I threw a monkey wrench into the festivities.

"They need me. I must go," I said.

Like a true Christian soldier, I assumed my self-righteous, martyr posture. Emma didn't try to resist me. She knew my frame of mind about these excursions.

Sure enough, I took the trip, and, for me, it rated amazing. Who wouldn't love the excitement of travel, meeting many new friends, and being the center of attention? My ministry time proved spiritually and mentally stimulating. Floating high like a kite while traveling back to Lima, I barely noticed the sixteen hours on rickety buses. Time flew by. This felt like cloud nine, having found my calling. God's Spirit affirmed His word preached at the meetings. We saw great results. The indigenous believers received help and thanked us for the instruction in righteousness. All seemed right with my world.

Then, I walked through our apartment door.

Although everyone at home showed joy at my return, something felt off about the whole scene. I sensed an untold back story. Fatigue caused me to gloss over it at the moment.

The bed called my name, and I disappeared for twelve hours. When I woke up the next day, my wife wasn't beside me.

Feeling a little groggy, I stumbled out to the kitchen and located my morning coffee. As I sat slumped over at the dining table, Emma passed by quietly. Soon, our ten-year-old son Joshua stood in front of me looking like he carried a message. His face summed things up, but he also had words to share.

"Dad, I know that this conference must have been important and everything, but next Thanksgiving, could you please stay home with us?"

The pain in his eyes taught me a valuable lesson about being there for my family. His broken heart at that moment still brings a tear, even after all these years. Like almost every minister I've met, there are regrets about choices made and the effects on our wife and children. Early in ministry experiences, preachers and teachers get eaten up with zeal. The thrill of following Jesus and helping others consumes time, energy, and our hearts. We can easily forget those closest to us who loved us before all the hoopla began.

I became a better dad and missionary because of the Thanksgiving miscue. I learned to put ministering to others in perspective. The family should have been my first place to minister. God gave me sweet Emma to help me understand priorities without judging me or becoming angry.

Despite the upset at home and my son's hurt feelings, I knew I'd found my calling.

*Yanesha Indians*
Peter Hocking is a legend in Peru and beyond. He is equal parts missionary and scientist, with a little hopeless eccentric thrown into the mix. Peter became one of my first contacts on the other side of the Andes. After the trip to the Thanksgiving conference, he invited me to a place in the high jungle,

where he'd set up a training camp with the Yanesha tribe. Peter commanded a lot of respect in Peru and gave me my first exposure to this friendly people group.

The son of missionaries, Peter grew up in Peru and inherited the legacy of his parents' wisdom and years of ministry. He had a deep interest in science and a bug collection that would be the envy of the Smithsonian Institution. Experts credit him with identifying new species of parrots and several other botany breakthroughs.

At the point I met him, he had built a base camp way out in the jungle. I brought a team of students from Venezuela who wanted to work with remote tribes. To access the Hocking/Yanesha facility, we first embarked on a twelve-hour bus trip from Lima to the town of Villa Rica. Next, we piled into a modified Toyota 4-wheel drive, extended-cab truck, with a pole mounted in the bed. Twenty people might crowd into the cab and the bed. We flew through the jungle, across streams and even rivers. Part of the modification package for these pickup trucks involved snorkel air filters. The trucks could venture into deeper water than a regular pickup without flooding out. The drivers knew the limits and tested them often, with water almost up to the windows and bed of the truck. We rode for ten hours over hills and through muddy swamps to get close enough to walk the rest of the way to the Yanesha area.

After the bouncy ride, we had to walk several hours to get over the last mountain. Exhausted from all that, we slogged up and down hills the final leg of our journey. Although a young man, I felt beat by the time we arrived.

Peter greeted us, and I introduced the team from Venezuela who came to help. They took in Peter's thin appearance, glasses, mustache, and receding hairline. Some might describe him as central casting's version of a jungle explorer.

The "camp" included a platform raised four feet off the

ground, covered by a thatched roof. We cooked on an open fire and washed our clothes and ourselves in the river.

Hocking sounded like a walking encyclopedia. He taught constantly as we worked through daily tasks at the base camp. I found him fascinating, though not great at social skills. At one point, when Peter was busy doing taxidermy on a giant grasshopper, I tried to make small talk, which I later learned he abhors.

"Peter, have you ever discovered any new species of insects?" I asked.

"With insects? That's for amateurs," he replied brusquely.

End of small talk conversation.

I bonded with a father of the Yanesha tribe named Alfredo. A believer, I could sense the spirit of God in Him and talked to him in Spanish about his relationship with Jesus. His paternal manner reassured me and mentored me concerning outdoor skills.

While the Venezuelan team cleared away underbrush to prepare for a fishing expedition, Alfredo led me to a spot in the nearby jungle. I depended on him to avoid getting bit by a snake or eaten by a large panther. First, we walked to a plant, and he dug it up. Showing me the peanut-like nuts on the bottom, he offered me some, and we ate them. Next, he dug up a different kind of vegetation, but cautioned me not to eat it. The fishermen would use the plant and its roots for an unusual style of fishing.

Alfredo beat on the barbasco plant to release its milky liquid. Then, he placed the plant and the milk in the river near a dam built by the Yanesha. The barbasco juice has a tranquilizing effect on armored catfish. Soon, these fish floated to the surface and collected into nets by the dam area. The Venezuelans and the Yanesha collected many fish, ranging in size from one-inch to five or six inches long.

A side benefit of this style of fishing was that other fish

come and feed off the armored catfish. The Yanesha men grabbed a few of the other fish, adding to our haul. The whole camp ate armored catfish for five or six days based on this one hunting trip.

When I became almost sick from eating so much armored catfish, Alfredo came walking through camp with a large electric eel he had killed. Expecting to have the eel for supper, I smiled throughout the afternoon. At dinnertime, we sat down to another meal of armored catfish. I asked Alfredo, "What's going on. I thought you caught an eel?"

"Oh, electric eels are filled with evil spirits," he said. "We can't eat that."

Despite his faith in Jesus, Alfredo retained a few beliefs from his pre-Christian days. I tried to retrieve the eel later that evening, but decay had already set in, and I could not eat it.

Alfredo and I spent much time together on that trip. We talked about many subjects, but the saddest involved his son.

"The Shining Path killed him. He refused to join them. I am proud of him, but my heart still aches from the loss."

"I'm so sorry, Alfredo. Is The Shining Path still a lot of trouble here?"

"Not so much. You saw the Army checkpoints. They are a deterrent to The Shining Path starting up again."

Although the terrorists' influence had waned by 2001, our group encountered several Peruvian Army checkpoints. The government must have still thought The Shining Path posed a threat.

The thatched roof over the platform needed replacing about every four or five years. Alfredo and Peter decided that our team could help them replace it, but this time using corrugated metal. The Venezuelans and I walked back over the mountain to collect the large sheets of metal at the place the Toyota trucks left us off. We carried the rope from the outpost because Alfredo knew we would need it to bind up the metal and make it easier to carry.

At the drop off point, we noticed an old building with a large, crudely drawn advertisement on the side. In Spanish, it said "Come in for a cold soda and crackers." The Venezuelans and I felt hot from our journey and realized we would soon turn around and go back with the metal.

"Alfredo, we brought no money with us into the jungle. Do you think they will give us some soda on our promise to pay them when the trucks come back for us? A soda pop would sure taste good about now."

"They might," Alfredo said. "I will go ask them."

Our guide disappeared into the store. After five minutes, he reappeared. We waited anxiously for the reply.

"I am so sorry. Mr. David. They say they are out of sodas."

"Well, they advertise crackers too. Maybe we could at least get a few crackers?"

"I will check," Alfredo said. Again, he disappeared into the store.

"I am sorry, Mr. David. They are out of crackers too."

We laughed sardonically. No truth in advertising, I thought.

Exhausted after hauling metal back to the camp, I stayed behind while the others hiked down to the river to bathe. As the sun descended beyond the horizon, my bath became more urgent. I found my way to a nearby stream and looked for an inviting place. Reaching the lowest point in the area, I climbed down into a cove and soaped up. As I began to relax, an unusual growling emanated from a bunch of bushes. The low-pitched sound and guttural purr sounded fierce. My mind raced. Looking around, it became obvious I'd selected the low ground, vulnerable to attack. A predator, like a panther, could jump down on me with little warning. Alone and unarmed, the situation felt desperate. In a mild panic, I collected my Ivory soap and ran back to camp carrying my clothes just as total darkness descended.

Before leaving, all of us hiked to church that Sunday morning. God saved a special treat for this part of our trip. Near one open area, we saw the most awe-inspiring blue butterflies. Their wingspan must have been between six or eight inches. When they flapped their wings, they rose two feet in the air. As thousands of them flapped again, they gracefully descended two feet. All across the way in front of us, we watched the most amazing blue dance of the butterflies.

*The Pichanaki Training Base Idea*
Not long after we moved to Peru, I got a call from a pastor in Pichanaki. Although beyond the Andes, Pichanaki is located just 383 kilometers from Lima, making it one of the closer outposts we visited.

"David, I have an amazing project for you. Pastor Barriger has long envisioned a training base in this area. One of my members donated a large parcel of land that would be perfect. The problem is time. I'm too busy to handle the details. Can you come out here to discuss it?"

Soon, I and another pastor from Comino de Vida church traveled by bus to Pichanaki. Details aside, the purpose sounded engaging. This pastor and I talked for hours, going over the possibilities and discussing how to navigate administrative hoops.

The man who intended to donate the parcel of land came from a wealthy family. His father, the first Mestizo to settle in that area, had made a great deal of money and controlled much land, not just this one parcel. The Peruvian government and this regional government required considerable paperwork, even for gifting acreage. I worked with others and filed the right papers. Things looked promising. Perhaps this longtime dream of Robert's would come true.

One summer day, a church colleague and I tagged along with the surveying crew and several members from the local area. With temperatures at 120 degrees in the sun, the heat took a toll on many of us. Since our roll seemed mainly ceremonial, I hoped it wouldn't take too long. While we watched the men work, an energetic boy, the son of a local pastor, seemed unusually animated. While he played and moved about oblivious to the furnace-like conditions, I stayed in the shade and exerted as little energy as possible.

Huddling near a group of trees with a few other men, I pointed out a large bees' nest overhead. As everyone gasped at the size of it, the energetic boy had other plans. He threw a large stick directly at the nest. It dislodged and fell to the ground splitting open near my feet. Before I could move, bees swarmed my face and began stinging me. Screaming, I fell to the ground and rolled as if trying to put out a fire in my clothing. When I gathered some semblance of composure, we all ran several yards away, swatting and flapping our arms. After calming down, one of the men approached me and stared at my face which must have looked like a pin cushion.

"You must have good blood," he said. "Otherwise, your eyes would be swollen shut by now."

Although always thankful for a compliment, his observation did little to make me feel better. He then proceeded to pull stingers from my body, one by one. After a while, I barely noticed the discomfort from his attempts to help. This qualified as a bad day on the mission field. I found another tree and sat down for a while. After the surveying ended, we headed back home to Lima. At least I'm not allergic became my only praise in that situation.

After many weeks and months of preparation and fund-raising, mostly by me, something disturbing happened. A group of squatters built small shacks on the property before the land transferred to the church's control. In Peru, the law is written to favor squatters. If they find unoccupied property and build even a small structure, it's difficult to reclaim the land and evict them.

Our benefactor found himself in a tough place. Either he would have to get the territorial police to come and evict the squatters or forget the whole matter. The previous time this landowner had done an eviction, the squatters later came to his family home with an angry mob. They fire-bombed his personal residence, and the inferno badly burned his wife. He decided he could not risk such a thing happening again.

My first high-profile project in Peru ended with a whimper as the benefactor withdrew his land offer. The training center vision, as well as three years of my time and effort, evaporated in an instant.

# 7

# Finding Miraculous Provision Everywhere

Back in Lima, Emma and I had enrolled our two oldest in a Christian school. Although the move to Peru required massive change for them, we trusted in the Lord and the resiliency of youth. We delivered them to their school each day, then continued on to a Christian ministry just on the outskirts of Lima. This ministry center sat strategically in a very poor part of town. Emma and I brought our youngest, Mary, with us to the mission each day. She would play in a corner as we worked, or she might just tag along with us as we did our assigned tasks.

Almost immediately, my wife and I found the hands-on

ministry work interesting and fulfilling. So much so, days came and went when the time got away from us. The work at this outreach center captured our full attention. One afternoon, we realized that we were late catching our bus back into the city. Worried that our two older children might get confused or feel forgotten, we dropped everything and hurried to pick them up across town.

While our children's welfare remained paramount to us, we also did not wish to aggravate their teacher. She openly shared her feelings that anyone who showed up late to get their children was showing disrespect to her. She honed a most intimidating stern look for tardy parents. (In those days, few people had personal cell phones, especially not struggling missionaries. So, we couldn't call and tell them we were on the way.)

Emma scooped up our youngest, Mary, and we hurried out the mission gate. Normally, we would walk about a mile to the main road to catch the bus to the children's school. We both felt rushed and stressed.

*Mystery Bus Number 9*
As usual, God had the whole thing under control. He used the circumstance to show us, once again, that He would take care of us in Peru. As soon as we stepped off the mission compound, we saw a small mini-bus coming up the dirt road. While unusual to see any traffic on this side road, we had never seen a city bus here. Yet, a bus, bounced along the rough terrain in our direction. The bus sputtered up to us, very much out of place, and Emma raised her hand to flag down the driver. Somewhat to our surprise, the bus skidded to a stop in the gravel and the driver let us hop aboard.

The only other people on the bus were a woman and child, who sat near to the driver. The woman occasionally talked to him in whispered tones, revealing a closeness that suggested she might be his wife. Emma and I sat comfortably with Mary, just a few rows back. We remarked how thankful we felt. We did not have to run the mile to the main road to catch our normal bus. As we bounced along, we soon discovered that the driver would not be stopping for any other passengers. We thought this mystery bus might be out of service, but where could the driver be going?

Although he did not have on a uniform, we missed this obvious clue when we first boarded. He looked like many of our regular bus drivers: mid-forties, stocky, big arms. Emma asked him the nature and destination of our ride. If we had boarded a bus going in the wrong direction, this would sink our already-delayed plan to pick up our other children.

"We noticed you aren't picking up anyone else," Emma said in Spanish, loudly enough for him to hear her over the sounds of the engine and road noise.

"I am taking the bus to a mechanic's shop for maintenance," he answered pleasantly.

"Oh, we need to get to our children's school," Emma replied, explaining the location where we needed to go.

"That's no problem," the driver said. "We are going right by there. I will let you out in front of the school."

Emma and I shot each other looks, like the ones people share when they realize a greater plan is afoot. Only Christians traveling in God's grace can understand the excitement of living for Jesus. Experiences like this bus from nowhere enlivened our love affair with God.

The normal bus fare would be two soles per passenger. In my spirit, I felt the Lord telling me to give the driver five soles for each of us. This generosity did not appeal to my frugal nature, so I figured two soles each would be adequate. Perhaps the generous thought came from my own thoughts and not God, I reasoned to myself. Although my efforts are always fruitless, I sometimes try to bargain with God. Just then, five-year-old Mary crawled from Emma's lap onto my own. I smiled at her amazing face. Without knowing my interior conversation about the bus fare, she looked up at me and said, "Daddy, I think you should give the driver five soles."

This became a teachable moment for me. It seemed that God wanted me to know his commitment to helping me stay on the right path. In my spirit, I repented of my momentary disobedient attitude. If he knew we needed a custom ride to our kids' school, God also knew the driver needed fifteen soles. Why had this not occurred to me before?

"God, I am so sorry, I will give him five soles each," I said out loud.

The mechanic shop turned out to be very near our kids' school. The driver dropped us off, just as he had promised. By not stopping to pick up anyone else, the bus made up the lost time. We arrived at the school before closing, thanks to our special bus ride arranged by the Lord. Everything we needed, the Father sent our way.

*Sharp Elbows and the Tamale Sales Girl*
When moving into a new mission assignment, the experts tell you there are three stages of adjustment:

Stage 1. Everything is great. Food tastes great. Everyone is nice. The new location is wonderful.

Stage 2. Reality stage. Honeymoon is over. You notice things that bug you.

Stage 3. Routine. You come to accept the good with the bad and adjust to a new normal. Little things stop bothering you.

One morning, I went to a bakery near our home in Lima. The bread, just fresh out of the oven, smelled like heaven. Still in stage two, I had developed a few pet peeves about Peruvian culture, at least the Lima version. One thing especially annoyed me. When standing in line, people would butt in front of me. Other shoppers had no problem jumping ahead in the queue during any brief lapses of attention. How rude!

The culture in the U.S. dictates you behave nicely to people you don't know. In Latin America, you are nice to people you know, but those you don't know become invisible to you. In Peru, the people at church and those we met elsewhere worked overtime to be kind to us. They knew us and treated us with the utmost respect. At the local bread store, standing in line could resemble playing in a pro basketball game: block out with your body and use sharp elbows to maintain your place in line.

There I stood, doing my best pro basketball player impression. Blocking out my rivals, I sought the freshest, most delectable bakery goods for our family. All the while, the luxurious smell of heavenly bread wafted in the air, making the wait almost insufferable.

On this day, my patience evaporated during a particularly long wait. With so many would-be interlopers, I developed an aggressive attitude about all the line butting going on ahead of me. When my turn finally arrived, I asked for five pieces of bread for one sol, about thirty cents. I purchased the bread and stomped out the door, dragging my now-less-than-sanctified attitude behind me.

As I exited, a cute little nina, about five years old, sweetly asked if I would like to buy some of her tamales to go with my bread. These street tamales had garnered quite a reputation and usually tasted delicious. Throw in the darling little saleswoman, and the tamales became an easy sale.

"I will take two tamales," I said in my most professional-sounding Spanish. As I fumbled for coins in my pocket, I noticed that she placed three tamales in a bag and handed them over. What?

With an overly stern look, I said, "I've asked for two tamales, young lady, and I will only pay you for two."

Meekly looking up amidst her dark curls, the child replied

in a gentle voice, "The third one is a gift because you're so nice."

My heart sank. I hurried away down the street, so she would not see the tears rolling down my face. God placed her in my path for good reason. I walked two blocks home, totally humbled and corrected by the Lord. He reminded me that my whole mission in Peru comprised loving people in the name of the Lord. I had to learn how to buy bread and tamales without losing my religion.

*Dodging Strikers in Pucallpa*
As we settled into new lives, I traveled deeper and deeper into the Amazon jungle. The topography of Peru made these trips interesting and challenging. Lima, on the Pacific Coast of South America, is set midway between Peru's northern and southern borders. The Andes Mountains run north and south, traversing not only Peru, but also four other countries. The Andes are visible from many of Peru's coastal towns and cities, creating amazing vistas. After traveling over the mountains, a long distance remains to reach the streams and rivers which connect to the Amazon. The terrain can be difficult and the journey long. First you come to mountain cities, then to the high jungle, and, at last, to the low jungle.

It might take sixty hours of bus rides, boating, and hiking to reach the most remote villages where we travelled. Some bus trips alone took thirty hours just to get halfway. The church in Lima breathed the same passion as I to reach remote people with the good news of the gospel. Although contacting indigenous people is not politically correct in some quarters, I know first-hand the misery of these people who don't yet know God.

Often, the villagers live in fear day and night. Their superstitions feed terrors around every natural occurrence. They create gods that must be appeased every time the river floods or a fire consumes one of their huts. Even the wind has a god that must receive one type of sacrifice or another. Teaching them about our loving Father brings relief of mind and soul. Seeing people released from the bondage of satanic fear is an amazing sight.

If we as Christians are not careful though, it's easy to give them one more easily angered god to appease. Over the years, many native Peruvians fell into ritualistic forms of Christianity. Instead of faith based on grace and the sacrifice of Jesus, some converts believe their salvation depends on various man-made activities and prescriptions for holiness. This isn't much better than the pagan worship they'd left behind. Those who Christ sets free are free indeed!

As I traveled across the Andes with trusted pastors from Lima, I became familiar with the churches on the eastern side of the mountains. These spiritual outposts served as natural staging areas for our trips further east into the rain forest. We developed contacts and good relationships with small and larger churches on the outskirts of civilization.

On one such an expedition, a team from Michigan wanted to join in a conference in the jungle city of Pucallpa. The name Pucallpa means red dirt, well titled since the founders built the city on red clay. As our trip approached, we heard of a big labor strike in Pucallpa that threatened to become violent. The pastor from Michigan asked me what he should do.

"The strike sounds dangerous," he said. "Do you think we should cancel our trip?"

After doing some checking, I responded, "Well, that's up to you. Regardless of whether you can go, I feel obligated to make the trip and speak there. I promised Pastor Fernando that I would come and share on several topics."

Our original team included eight to ten people from Michigan. After consulting with their team, he decided that only two of his men should take part. The rest stayed behind and helped with ministry activities in Lima.

The three of us flew out to Pucallpa, trusting in the Lord to protect us. When we arrived, Pastor Fernando and at least half of his congregation came to the airport as a welcoming party. What an awesome greeting!

Because of the strike, no taxis patrolled the airport. Only a fool would take a motor vehicle out onto the streets and risk damage to his car and himself. Strikers had thrown glass and other debris onto many of the small streets and blocked off the larger boulevards. Protesters burned tires, and the smell of burnt rubber hung in the air as we walked from the airport. Our peculiar procession met no resistance as we paraded through nearby neighborhoods. After a hefty walk, we arrived at the pastor's home near the church. Our visit felt a little like reinforcements flying into a war zone to bolster the troops.

Rustic might be an understatement. Pastor Fernando's residence did not include running water. We saw only an outhouse to do our business.

Despite many reports of trouble throughout the city, the strike did not cancel or even slow down our Christian conference. Three times a day, we walked from the house to the church, about one mile away. Morning, afternoon, and evening sessions drew sizable crowds. The other two men and I enjoyed our roles as teachers and prayer warriors during the conference. The praise, worship and teaching seemed specially blessed, perhaps because of the difficult conditions caused by the strike.

Although the locals may have been used to it, the ninety-degree temperatures and high humidity sapped us gringos. By the time we got to the church or back to the pastor's home, we ended up covered from head to toe in sweat and red dust from the clay.

As we passed strikers out on the street, we put our heads

# Finding Miraculous Provisions Everywhere

down, eyes glued to the dirt road ahead of us. Knowing that angry mobs often react poorly to strangers. we did not want to stick out as foreigners.

On the last afternoon of the three-day conference, the men from Michigan and I marched happily back to the pastor's house, rejoicing at all the Lord had accomplished. With no warning, we came upon a throng of people carrying sticks and big pots and pans. A few held up computer components as if rejoicing to the tech gods. The group looked more menacing and angrier than the other strikers we had encountered that week. With God's help, we slipped past the strikers and found our way to relative safety at the pastor's home.

*Mangos and Murder*

As we sat in the backyard, the pastor's wife peeled large, fragrant mangoes for each of us to eat. The fruit looked and smelled amazing. Before I could dig in, the pastor's oldest son, about seventeen years old, ran into the backyard, speaking excitedly.

"It's the craziest thing," he shouted. "They ransacked the university and killed one of the security guards. A mob has taken the university director hostage. Tomorrow, my friend said they plan to march on the airport and ransack it too."

"But we fly back to Lima tomorrow," I said. Dejection washed over me and the other Spanish speakers close enough to hear.

The pastor's wife stood there listening, holding a large butcher knife and a mango. She stared at me with concern, furrowing her brow. In Spanish, she said "Oh, I hope they don't take you three as hostages."

A sinking feeling enveloped my stomach. Debating whether to interpret her comments for the two English-speaking Michigan guys, I looked over at one of my traveling companions. With comic timing, he yelled "David, you must try this mango! It's the sweetest thing I've ever tasted!"

His comment reminded me of my young children. When I would worry about something, they played quietly, blissfully ignorant of any danger. I decided that, in this case, ignorance would remain bliss for my Wolverine friends. I could think of no reason to worry them when we had no control over the situation, so I committed the matter to the Lord in prayer. All I could do would be trust and put our safety in His capable hands.

That evening, our American trio walked to the closing service of the conference, praying the whole way as we went. I begged for the Lord's protection. My friends prayed for God's Spirit to continue the miraculous move we had experienced throughout these meetings.

Everything went well. God's Spirit blessed; people were healed; and we enjoyed everything from the opening worship song to the last prayer of repentance at the altar. Civil insurrection does not intimidate the Lord. His program goes forward despite the enemy's antics or my fears.

Following the service, I prayed my way back to the pastor's house. Despite nervousness, sleep came within just a few minutes.

Bam! In the middle of the night, a gigantic thunderclap awakened me. A huge storm blew in out of nowhere and abundant rains descended, blanketing the city in a tremendous volume of water. I smiled to myself as I lay in bed, wondering what the Lord may do for us.

In those days, many of the city streets remained unpaved. The rain brought the whole city to a near standstill. Regular activities ceased. No one without urgent business wanted to go out when the red mud filled the streets.

Happy as larks, my two Michigan companions and I dragged our bags through the abandoned streets to the airport. We saw no one on the impassable, mud-caked streets.

It kept raining, and we felt soaked to the bone by the time we arrived, without incident, at the airport. We did not see a single protester. Wondering if our flight would take off on the normal schedule, we checked in at the counter. While cloud cover prevented some planes from leaving that morning, we prayed with great fervor for God's help. Almost miraculously, the clouds parted just in time, and our plane from Lima landed. As soon as the airline employees finished servicing the aircraft, we scampered aboard, and the plane took off for Lima on time. God provided for us every step of the way on that trip. It just took a little courage and determination to keep our commitment.

During those turbulent times, the government did not seem to take strikes seriously until someone lost their life. A college security guard died before the people on both sides settled the strike. Soon after, the government restored order, and things returned to normal in Pucallpa.

*Strike Two–Should Have Learned My Lesson*
After my experience in the first labor strike, I did not take away any lesson about canceling in the face of adversity. Others may find it prudent if there is an inkling of a strike; stay far away until they resolve the unrest. In my defense, authorities and protesters announced the Juliaca strike would end at 6:00 p.m. on the day of our flight. A couple from Denver planned to come along with me, each expressing excitement about our mission. As scheduled, we flew into Juliaca before heading to our final destination of Puno.

Both cities rest high in the Andes, around 13,000 feet above sea level. We could fly most of the way, avoiding the long bus trip. However, the air travel to such an elevated destination had a side effect. Our first steps off the plane in Juliaca told us we weren't in Lima any more.

My legs felt heavy, and I found breathing difficult. Although my guests for this trip hailed from Denver, another high-altitude city, they felt the same symptoms. Though they call Denver the mile-high city, it rests only 5,280 feet above sea level, a third as high as Juliaca. My traveling companions noticed several symptoms of altitude sickness upon arrival. We ambled to the luggage carousel to retrieve our bags. After more walking at a measured pace, we met up with the van driver who planned to drive us from Juliaca to Puno.

While the strike in this region had "officially" ended, our driver saw a great deal of debris on his way to pick us up. Apparently, some rioters missed the memo about the strike ending. On the positive side, our driver knew less-traveled avenues and alleyways. We sped along side streets at a healthy clip. We felt good about our progress. Before we got all the way out of Juliaca, the van slowed way down and seemed to stop for no reason.

"Is something going on?" I asked from the backseat, while nervously tapping my fingers on the arm rest.

"There are kids blocking the road ahead," our van driver answered in Spanish.

Along with our chauffeur, the owner of the van joined us for the two-hour trip to Puno. She sat on the passenger side up front, chiming in with a play-by-play: "Kids are playing volleyball. They've stretched their net across the street, and we can't get through." Then, she turned to the driver and barked, "Get out and talk to them. We need to keep going." This woman seemed experienced at leading and directing others. I suspected that she wouldn't be easily intimidated.

The driver dutifully jumped out of the van and hustled toward the young people. A girl, taller than the others, aggressively stepped to the fore and appeared to be speaking belligerently to the driver. Partly from her loud voice and partly from her hand motions, we could tell she wanted him to go around to different street. Though he attempted to get her to change her mind, she defiantly shook her head. The driver walked back to the van with his head down.

As he told us what the girl said, the owner became incensed. "If she refuses to take down the net, just drive right through it," she demanded. "Get going!"

The driver did as commanded. He floored the van and drove right down the middle of the street with children jumping aside for their lives. He did not pause as we impacted the net and snapped it from its tethers. Off we went, the volleyball net flapping on both sides of our van. The young people yelled and shook their fists at us as we passed them. In time, the net migrated to the roof, snagging on the luggage carrier. We must have been quite a sight as we escaped from Juliaca.

We drove the rest of the way out of town without further incident. On our drive to Puno, we saw scenes that suggested the strike had ended. Roads mostly looked clear, and people swept up debris in a few spots where there must have been trouble. Everything appeared quiet, or at least returning to normal. Then, somewhere between Puno and Juliaca, we saw people standing in the road and large obstacles strategically placed to stop traffic. According to our driver, he knew of no back streets we could take to avoid this section of roadway.

"It looks like people are feeling their whiskey muscles after drinking all day," the van owner said snidely. I admired her strength and courage but hoped she did not get us into a physical altercation. As for me and the couple from Denver, we claimed to be lovers of souls and not fist fighters.

"This is the only road, and people are blocking it," the driver said. He gave his boss a worried look, perhaps fearing that she would order him to drive through the riotous mob up ahead.

An imposing group stood their ground, chanting in Spanish, "The strike is not over!" and "No one is getting through here!" Unlike the young people we encountered in Juliaca, this mob had several good-size men and women with makeshift weapons like large planks of wood and metal rods.

Several cars, coming from the other direction, had stopped in a line, but our van had no other cars as a buffer. We sat first in line coming from Juliaca. From time to time, a demonstrator hurled a rock or two in our general direction. When we didn't turn back, they lit on fire small stands of grass on the side of the road, moving ever nearer our van.

"The smoke is making my eyes burn," I said.

"This isn't good for breathing," the driver added.

At that altitude, the night sky commonly turns a brilliant array of colors. Far from any light pollution, I had seen every detail of the Milky Way on a previous trip. This time, the smoke obscured everything. If the strike had ended earlier, we wouldn't have been in this predicament.

The whole scene spiraled out of hand. The chanting intensified and more rocks sailed through the air, some bouncing on the van's roof. We instinctively put our arms over our faces and heads to shield ourselves, though none of the rocks penetrated the van.

My Denver friends processed the situation through their U.S. frame of reference. The pastor's wife compared everything to what she knew from Denver. Her first time in another country, I could excuse her attitude. Nevertheless, her comments proved unhelpful.

"Why don't these people protest off the roadway?" she said. "We would still know their grievances without stopping people from traveling. Also, why don't they at least pick up their own trash? Somebody will need to come out here and clean up after them. So irresponsible."

With the inconveniences of the day and tiredness, her mood grew darker. Embarrassed as she degraded the Peruvian way of doing things over and over, I knew she wasn't making a good impression on our driver or the owner of

### Finding Miraculous Provisions Everywhere

the van. My patience with the situation ran out as fear and fatigue overtook my better nature. Such a difficult spot, and my guest didn't understand that complaining got us nowhere.

The people alongside the road grew more and more agitated until they had worked up quite a lather. On two occasions, drivers coming from the Puno direction drove right through the mob. Several rioters threw heavy stones at them and beat on the offending vehicles. Each time, the drivers made their way through the pack of rioters, but their vehicles suffered severe damage. The busted-up windows and large dents worried my traveling companions, as we watched those vehicles limping past our position.

I felt scared, not just for myself, but for the four traveling with me. Perhaps all of us prayed silent prayers for God's help, but I know I prayed extra fervently.

Out of the blue, we heard loud footsteps. Police from Juliaca, clad in full riot gear, marched up beside our van. In an amazing show of force, they had come to break up the strike. They looked impressive in sharp uniforms and carrying batons.

"We're saved" the van owner shouted. "The riot police from Juliaca are here! They will teach those hombres a thing or two."

The three of us in the backseat cheered with great gusto. An instant later, the rioters charged toward the police. To our surprise and mild horror, the police turned and ran in the opposite direction, leaving us even more exposed to the now-incensed mob.

"The police are running for their lives" the pastor's wife said, with panic in her voice. "This is so irregular."

I let out a slight horse laugh at the naiveté of her statement and turn of phrase. Then, my mood sobered as I saw the mob of rioters surrounding our van. We were in deep trouble.

Before the unholy assembly had time to think about

attacking us, police from Puno arrived from the other direction. They fired tear gas into the crowd surrounding our van. Although glad to see the reinforcements, our tears of joy soon mixed with tears from the toxic gas. Considerable moisture flowed down our cheeks as we praised the Lord and winced in pain. I laughed and cried at the same time.

In minutes, the trouble ended, and the crowd dispersed. We continued on our way, dodging debris in the road, the volleyball net still flapping in the breeze.

## On the Shores of Lake Titicaca

Puno spreads majestically along the shores of Lake Titicaca, the highest navigable lake in the world. Flat and windy, the high plains around Lake Titicaca rest at 12,420 feet above sea level. It took two days for our bodies to adjust to the altitude and all of our dizziness to subside. Even the visitors from Denver labored to breathe.

In such lofty air, the sun can do great damage to human skin. Many of the indigenous children have scars on their faces where the sun ravaged capillaries. Despite the harsh effects, the ancient Incas revered the sun as their god. They believed the first Inca arose from Lake Titicaca at sunrise and created the Inca Empire.

The study of anthropology fascinates me. As I contemplate their belief system, I can see why they might believe the sun is god. When the sun is out, the climate is pleasant. But on cloudy days, the high-altitude environment is harsh and unforgiving. Many modern-day Quechuas still believe in the sun god. They celebrate special festivals and perform a variety of rituals to keep their sun god happy.

Although a difficult journey to Puno, my visitors settled in and expressed gratitude for my help in getting us to the region. We drank in the unique topography and beautiful scenery. The Denver pastor's father had died in a plane crash in this area, some forty years earlier. Emotional and spiritual, his pilgrimage retraced what he knew of his father's steps. As their guide for this portion of the trek, many things came into perspective for me. Many emotions came to the surface for this man and his wife.

Our conference presentations drew positive reviews. Our gracious hosts and the members at the local church treated us as old friends. Like many of our sessions, the local clergy had requested leadership training. We used books by John Maxwell and other curricula to reinforce biblical principles. We shared strong management paradigms to help with leadership and administration of their local churches. Seeing faces light up brightened everyone's mood, as we shared various strategies for overcoming challenges.

At night, temperatures plummeted. The rain made us miserable. Our modest lodging place included strategic leaks. We listened to a symphony of rhythmic plopping all night. To survive, we slept under three or four heavy Alpaca blankets. Used since Inca times, Alpaca wool serves as a super insulator. Individually, the animal's fine fibers help very little, but the wool becomes dense when woven together into blankets or coats. Trust me, Alpaca blankets provide superior insulation properties under the worst conditions.

Trying to sleep in the extreme altitude mimics sleep apnea. Many times, we woke up gasping for breath due to the thin air and the intense weight of the heavy blankets. After three days, the ministry sessions refreshed our souls, but our bodies left the area beaten up by the lack of breathable air. Before it ended, I praised God for the trip and for including these new friends from Denver. When we returned to sea level, I praised Him even more for the gift of normal breathing–a forgotten gift I had never appreciated so much.

# 8

# Swashbuckling Through the Jungle

Visitors from the United States warmed our hearts and eased homesickness. Unaccustomed to South American culture, they proved easy marks for good-natured jesting. Multiply that by one hundred when we traveled away from the major metropolitan city of Lima. Primitive surroundings and lack of creature comforts appear off-putting at first. For those of us accustomed to the inconveniences, we found a certain amount of humor in messing with our visiting friends, although we had similar reactions when we first experienced large insects or oppressive heat. We enjoyed watching newbies adjust to these mini-perils.

On occasions when we dined on a plate of monkey meat or grub worms, why not throw in a comment like bon Appetit? The meal might be our host's most precious delicacy, so turning down the food or making a face would be the worst of insults. That is Missionary 101 training. To reject a person's offering of food insults his or her dignity, and it rejects their culture.

The gospel mission comes before personal likes and dislikes. After a long day of traveling, my companions would be hungry by dinnertime. Before the trip, I insisted that they remove all American snacks from their bags and leave such food behind in Lima. Monkey tastes much better when you face hunger and have no other choices.

Some people groups living deep in the jungle practice a unique custom to determine whether visitors deserve a warm welcome. Cassava root is a staple in the native diet. They boil it and make a beverage called masato. It includes chewing a boiled root and spitting it back out. Then, tribesmen let the cassava and spit ferment for a few days. As they hand a visitor a gourd of masato, the village elders observe whether the visitor readily accepts and consumes it. How the guest treats the offering of masato determines how the tribe treats the guest himself.

Masato is not for the faint of heart and demands a step of faith. We had to rely on the words of Jesus when He said, "when they drink deadly poison, it will not hurt them at all" (Mark 16:18). Though not necessarily deadly, it is hardly a health drink.

Malaria is another problem in the deep jungle. One week, while hosting a medical team from California, we visited a village where three-quarters of the people suffered from malaria. The wetlands can be so beautiful and yet so full of danger. Mosquitoes and other biting insects multiply there. These bloodsuckers carry active malaria and other serious diseases. The bugs stay hungry for blood from five in the evening until five the next morning.

One day, after attending to all the ambulatory villagers at our makeshift clinic, we traveled hut-by-hut to take care of those too sick to come to us. One fellow lay on a mat outside his hut, hair soaked from fever, shaking from the ravages of malaria. After administering medication, we took him by the hand and prayed with him. You know how sometimes you pray with one eye open? Well, this became one of those times for me. I glanced at my watch and noticed the time, five o'clock. I also noticed mosquitoes biting this poor fellow, and then buzzing over to my hand.

My prayers became animated and even a little Pentecostal as I waved and shook my arms, mainly to ward off the mosquitoes. Somehow, the Lord kept me from getting malaria despite many such trips into the jungle.

Most of my ministry up to at this point included difficult travel. As I mentioned before, one trip might take thirty hours just to get over the Andes and into the jungle. With everything so distant and with the laborious travel, there remained another climate-induced barrier. Some areas of Peru become accessible only during the rainy season. One place we needed to go was on the Yanayacu river, an off-shoot from the Amazon. We reached the area by boat during the jungle's rainy season. The indigenous people, for all intents and purposes, have access to the rest of the world only six months of the year. The alternative during the rest of the year would be an endless slog through snake-infested jungle trails and knee-deep mud.

## *Parinari*

During one of my first years back in Peru, we paddled into a town called Parinari. Taking clothing and food, we taught classes each evening. Although remote, this church had a generator. The village itself had no electricity except for the church's one generator. Absent other options, church activities became the go-to nighttime activity. The people had nothing else to do after dark. Everyone in the village came out to hear the teachers from far away.

A friend from San Diego, Bruce Balcombe, agreed to come along on this trip. He taught at the church in Lima but lacked experience going this far out into the sticks. As we worshiped that night, he and I waited for our turn to take the podium. In the blink of an eye, the biggest rat I've ever seen crawled up the wall on the stage. Fortunately, the band played on, not noticing. I turned to see Bruce's expression. His eyes grew as wide as pingpong balls.

"Did you see the size of that rat?" Bruce asked. He looked and sounded a little nauseous. He must have realized that his turn on the stage would soon arrive, meaning he might be just a few feet from the hefty rodent.

"Wait until you see the size of the anaconda chasing it," I replied.

Bruce's eyes expanded even larger, more like the size of soccer balls.

We saw a menagerie of wildlife out in the jungle. I can't describe my joy and amazement the first time I saw fresh-water dolphins, capybaras (the world's largest rodent which stands as tall as a goat), and the endless number of brightly adorned exotic birds. So much fun...

### Boat Troubles on the Paranapuã

The Chiahuitas captured my heart and became one of the most beloved partners in my gospel mission in Peru. Because of their sweet spirit and interest in Bible training, we regularly endured the thirty-five-hour trips to reach them. Then, we made our way to the jumping off place into the river system from which we accessed their village. On one trip, two American fellows came along with us. One hailed from Los Angeles and the other, Jordan, came from New York City. Both provided great companionship and showed excitement about the adventure.

Once at the river, we used hollowed-out canoes and small motors called peque-peques, named by the locals after the sound they make: peque, peque, peque. The motor's long tail sits right on the surface of the water and works well for rivers that often become shallow in places. A traditional outboard motor would drag the bottom and rip to pieces in the mud and vines. A trade-off is that traditional outboard motors are much more powerful and make the boat faster than peque-peques.

The night before our planned departure, we awakened to flashes of lightening in the distance. If it also had rained as much upstream, we knew the current might be strong against us. Jordan and I rode in one canoe with two men and a group of Shipibo Indian women. These young Shipibo ladies were gifted in praise and worship. They incorporated native cultural dances into their worship of Jehovah. It is the equivalent to writing hymns with the tune of a modern song, like John Wesley and others have done throughout church history. It makes worship more accessible and eliminates cultural barriers. Can you imagine if someone asked you to learn some complicated classical music with lyrics in another language to worship a God you had only just come to know?

Our plan for this trip included teaching a distant tribe (the Chiahuitas) about worship. We wanted them to know they did not have to abandon all aspects of their culture to worship the one, true God. The Shipibo women came along in full dancing costumes to show the Chiahuitas how to use dance in worship. The Shipibo outfits included feathers and brightly dyed fabrics. We must have been a sight as we came into view of their village.

As we made our way upriver, two Chiahuitas brothers manned the front and back of the boat, guiding us on the way to their village. The man in back controlled the peque-peque. The man in front used a large pole to free us from low points and to keep us from running ashore. With the overnight rain, we encountered several places where the current became too strong. The small engine struggled carrying five men and the Shipibo dance troupe.

Big trees came floating down the middle of the river, so we had to dodge back and forth to keep from being wiped out as these mega projectiles barreled downriver. Although the wood canoes are stable enough, there are substantial risks if they capsize. More than a few people have lost their lives when these heavy boats turned over in turbulence. The weight of an overturned canoe of this type can trap several people under the water, pinning them to the river bottom.

With the small motor fighting the heavy current, we made almost no progress. Worse yet, blood-sucking mosquitoes and other bugs swarmed us. Under normal currents, the peque-peque-powered canoe can outrun the bugs, but not on this day. With everyone miserable from the heat and the bugs, we looked for a place to stop for lunch, hoping the swiftest currents might pass while we ate. Although there are great fluctuations in the volume of water on the river, flow returns to normal soon after the rain stops.

We headed to a riverbank which looked like a good spot to put in. The Chiahuita brother in the front used a long pole, attempting to guide us to shore. When he exited the boat near the riverbank, a big rush of water came along and sucked the boat and the rest of us across the river. Our steering mechanism now gone, we had no choice but to go where the current drove us. When we reached the far side, the boat fell into peril, nearly getting wiped out by the current. The flow of the river dangerously rocked us from side to side.

"Jordan, help me," I yelled as I grabbed roots, and anything else to get a hold on the muddy riverbank. "We are about to capsize!" I screamed.

It quickly became a life or death struggle. I fought against the tide, trying desperately to save our lives. The Shipibo ladies saw the precariousness of our predicament and jumped ship. They nimbly hopped out and climbed onto the branches of an overhanging tree. They must have posed an interesting sight, moving about so nimbly in their feathers and tribal garb. The remaining Chiahuita brother in the boat's rear regained some degree of control and guided us back toward the other side of the river.

"Jordan, why did you only sit there sheltering your camera," I asked. "We might have died."

"If I lost the camera, my wife would have killed us both, anyway. This camera is expensive," he said sheepishly as the current and peque-peque took us back across the river where we had parted company with our pole man.

No sooner did we get there than the Shipibo girls began yelling to us in their language. "The ants are biting us. Help us. This is unbearable."

With our helmsman back on board, we traversed the river one more time and maneuvered into position. The Shipibo girls nimbly leapt back aboard. All this action took over an hour, dealing with the mayhem as it unfolded. With everyone exhausted, we collapsed on the beach at the spot we originally picked out. After a little break, we unloaded the food and found a place in the grass. We ate lunch, and it rejuvenated us. We enjoyed our break time and the nourishing food. As we rested, our guide checked out conditions on the river. The water had receded to a safer level. We all climbed back in the boat and resumed our journey. The bright sun beat down on us, but we laughed and talked as we went.

*An Interesting Proposition*
The missionaries from New York and LA asked many questions about Amazonian wildlife. On the slow-going boat trip, we found plenty of time to talk about the animals, among other topics. Jordan wondered about the dangers of the river, such as caimans and anacondas. Jordan smiled as I pointed out a few caimans and some parrots as we passed.

When we arrived at the village where we planned to spend the night, I told my fellow travelers to do as they liked, but I planned to go back down to the river to get a bath. Nothing energized me like sleeping in the jungle, but only after bathing away the day's grime and sweat. With soap and towel in hand, I made a beeline to the river.

"Aren't there snakes in the river?" Jordan asked.

"No, no snakes," I replied.

"What about alligators?" his companion asked.

"No, no alligators," I peeled off my shirt and waded into the water.

As I lathered up, I pretended that something grabbed me from underneath the water. I put on my best show of pretending to wrestle a caiman. My friends did not take a single step in my direction. After holding my breath for several seconds, I gave up my pretense and came up for air.

"Fine friends you turn out to be. I might have drowned," I said, playfully splashing water in their general direction.

"We had to survive all this so we could tell your wife what happened to you," Jordan replied.

*Chiahuita Village*
The next day, we worked the rest of the way upriver to the little Chiahuita village. Tribesmen and women watched intently as the Shipibo girls showed how they do their style of worship. At the meetings, we taught lessons prepared in Spanish, and someone translated into Chiahuita. This

ministry requires great faith. We believe in the power of God's word and the power of His Spirit to apply the teaching to their hearts. We have faith that our sacrifice in coming out to these distant places made a positive impact. God's love inhabits the Christian's mind and spirit. Only His love gave us the strength to show up and care for people with whom communication only came with difficulty. In our fleshly selves, such sacrifice is impossible, but empowered by God, great compassion becomes possible and even inevitable.

As a rule, the men spoke both their native language and some Spanish. However, their wives spoke only Chiahuita. This sometimes gave the husbands an upper hand when dealing with strangers. At least, they thought they had an upper hand over their wives.

One of the Chiahuita brothers expressed an interest in my watch. The men liked to barter with visitors. I loved to collect little crowns that the village elders wore. Often crafted out of lovely colored parrot, toucan or macaw feathers, the crowns bring back the reality of being out in the jungle.

The last time I had visited the Chiahuita village, I traded my then-current watch for this same brother's crown. Now, six months later, he recognized me and wanted to do another trade.

"Will you trade me this crown for your watch," he asked, pointing to his head.

"No, this is a much better watch," I said. "That crown is not as good as the last one you gave me in exchange for my less-expensive watch."

"The other watch you sold me no good," he insisted. "It stopped working a short time after you left."

In the jungle conditions, the watch did not hold up well. Anyone with knowledge of modern watches would have seen the risk in such a hot, damp environment. The tribesman intuited that the little crown he wore did not impress me.

The man's wife wore a necklace made of polished native seeds. Her stunning jewelry looked intricate and geometric. She must have spent hours creating the necklace.

"The crown doesn't interest me, but your wife's necklace looks good," I said.

The wife, who did not speak Spanish, saw me pointing toward her necklace. She looked at me disapprovingly and shook her head no, throwing in a disgusted grimace for good measure. Having worked many days to create that sweet necklace, she had no plan to give it up for another shiny toy for her husband. Perhaps the woman wondered, this far out, who cares about the time anyway?

The man turned in my direction and, with a straight face, said, "She says yes."

I laughed, realizing he was telling a boldface lie. The situation struck me funny as it spoke volumes about the couple's marital relationship. Ill-advisedly, I continued. "I would not want her to come after me with a frying pan," I said.

His response taught me once again that humor doesn't translate well when working with remote tribes. My joke fell flat between the language and cultural barriers.

"You want to trade for a frying pan instead?" he asked, looking confused.

Although I never got that necklace, I relented and traded the man my watch for some other tribal keepsakes. I still feel fondness for those people and treasure the small mementos they traded.

In this remote Chiahuita village, the people lived with few material belongings. Their simple life created challenges in relating the gospel message. For example, money meant little to them. We gave substantial thought and prayer to make the lessons relevant to people in each specific society.

They had no electricity. A single Coleman lantern hung from a hook on the ceiling of the school house, where we held our meetings. As the night wore on, the lamp would grow dim. Someone would pull out a table, climb up, and pump up the lantern while the teacher continued to speak. While this went on, all eyes turned to the "lantern man" with no one paying attention to the message. Except for the school, the village houses sat on platforms with just a roof, no sides to the structures. The platforms, three feet off the ground, yielded protection against snakes and the wet ground. With no walls, the villagers expected no privacy from each other and gave none in return.

The three of us slept in one room of the school. For a thousand reasons, we became an instant curiosity to the Chiahuitas. The whole time we spent in the village, men followed us everywhere and watched our every move. We posed curious sights, no doubt. Our clothes, our mannerisms, and our speech were foreign to them. Perhaps they viewed us with anthropological interest, studying the strange habits of the Western-descended male.

At one point, Jordan freaked out at their constant gazing. As we settled down to sleep, several men stood staring through the open windows and door of the school. Jordan yelled at the men in English, "What are you staring at? Go away."

After he chased them off, he said, "I feel like an animal in the zoo."

I smiled, knowing how fascinated many Westerners must have been over the centuries when looking at tribesmen. Reversing the circumstances held a certain poetry.

*Face Paint*
When a tribe is first contacted, a common practice is to ask a neighboring tribe for help with introductions. We would go to one tribe that had already accepted us and Christ, then we invited them to accompany us to meet the new tribe. A potential pitfall lurked in the midst of this plan. Neighboring

tribes often call the uncontacted tribe by a not-so-nice name, like "stinky people" or "goofy tribe." For example, their neighbors called the Ashaninkas "campas," which means "the grubby ones."

From time to time, this led to hilariously bad results for Christian mission efforts. For example, a well-known non-profit organization printed a Bible using a bad name. Neighboring tribes of the Yaneshas had dubbed them the Amoeshas, translated as "the dummies." For years, the Amoeshas' Bible sported the label, "Dummy's Bible." Since that time, they have corrected the name of the tribe and their Bible. Before we left, the Chiahuitas wanted to show us their affection and strengthen our growing relationship with them. On our last night in the village, we heard whispering all around us while the men of the tribe signaled with sweeping hand motions and exaggerated facial expressions.

"What's going on?" Jordan asked, nervously scratching his head

"I am not sure. Everything is going well. They were happy a few minutes ago. We have to trust God and keep smiling."

The Chiahuita chief told us that the time had arrived for him to initiate us. They pulled out knives, causing the three of us not just a little concern. We did not understand what they planned to do with their sharp-looking knives. Despite our apprehension, the warriors brought out a large container of what appeared to be walnuts. Those holding the knives used them to cut off the outer shell of the nuts.

"Just stand still," I told Jordan, who looked as if he might bolt into the jungle at any moment. The men spread huito juice on our faces, painting distinctive black lines that outlined our facial features. They transformed us into Amazonian warriors.

After the solemn ceremony, I took one of the Chiahuitas aside. The honor given us represented a significant step in our relationship. At the same time, I wondered about a practical matter.

"Will this huito juice wash off soon," I asked, trying to seem polite and nonchalant.

"It will wear off before you know it," the tribesman said. He smiled and nodded.

We looked every bit the part of Chiahuita warriors, and we felt great emotion that they considered us worthy of this honor. We slept well that night under the Amazon moon. The people of the jungle heard our message about Jesus and welcomed us into their inner circle. We became one with the Amazon, if only for a night.

*Nice View of the River*
After a two-week visit with the Chiahuitas, we longed for non-tribal food. Chiahuita cuisine lacks variety and got old after a few days. We appreciated their hospitality, but our appetites wanted a good, American meal ... or at least a decent Peruvian coastal meal.

The day grew long as we continued farther back up the river. Even though we were now going with the current, travel took considerable time in the heavy canoes. As soon we reached the town of Yurimuaguas, we intended to head out to the best restaurant in town and consume a great meal. We hurried from the boat dock and hailed a three-wheeled taxi. With great anticipation, we sought the first decent restaurant to chow down.

"Where is the best restaurant in town?" I asked, my mouth already watering.

"You will love it," our driver replied. "The food tastes magnificent. None better in town. The best part is the view as the eatery sits on a cliff overlooking the river."

Jordan gave me the look, and I knew what he was thinking.

"Hmm, no thank you," the three of us said, almost in unison.

"We have spent too much time on the river, and we are looking for something far from the riverbank," I said with a smile. My companions laughed, letting out a hoot in agreement.

Our driver changed course and took us to a modest family restaurant. We overdid it with a huge meal of greasy food. In the moment, it seemed like an appropriate attempt to assuage our hunger, but the massive quantity of oily food made me sick before the night concluded. Perhaps it was nature's way of telling me to appreciate the simple food of the Chiahuitas.

Little did we know; walnut juice does not quickly wear off. Once back to Lima and civilization, we received strange looks and stares from many passersby. Emma just laughed when she took her first look at me. Through the experience, we learned the hard way that it takes weeks for the huito to wear off. We tried rubbing alcohol, nail polish remover, and several kinds of soap. Huito juice is durable stuff. While quite an honor from the tribe, we felt embarrassed to walk around Lima with the painted faces of Amazon warriors.

In some ways, my huito face became a metaphor for this period of my missionary service. My body returned to Lima's polite society, but my heart stayed in the Amazon jungle. God knit me together with the people beyond the Andes. Until my next trip, I stayed homesick for the indigenous people. I missed the many adventures of the big river.

Later, the Chiahuitas got a new name. Now they are called the Shauwi.

# 9

# El Friaje (Without a Jacket)

For about three days each year, the Peruvian Amazon becomes frigid. During that short time, the wind changes and blows up from the deep south, Bolivia and Argentina. The rest of the year, the jungle temperatures run from hot to insanely hot. I had heard about these San Juan winds but had not experienced them. After another invigorating bus ride through the Andes, my traveling companions and I came to the western mountainous region known as the high jungle. We intended to travel on to the eastern flatland low jungle. The high and low jungles are so named based on altitude.

As we stopped in the high jungle town of Satipo, we

recognized that this would be the last town of any size before we moved into less populated areas. The next day, a taxi would take us three hours down to the river. The weather ran colder than usual. While we had time, I headed to the local market and found a woman selling light jackets.

As usual in the negotiating system common to these markets, I first talked nonchalantly about the jacket I liked. The trick is don't show too much interest but express a casual regard for the product and note a positive aspect of the item.

"How much for that jacket; it seems of respectable quality?" I asked in my best local Spanish accent.

"Thirty soles," the artful businesswoman said.

Although I could afford the price, which equated ten dollars at the exchange rate, I knew negotiation often came with the territory.

"I will give you twenty-five soles," I said. I had sprung my trap! She may have thought I represented some naïve outsider, but behind my gringo face lies a shrewd negotiator. No pride here, just amazing self-confidence. At least, that's what I told myself.

She stared at me, expressionless, and said, "No. The price is thirty soles."

Who did this woman think she was dealing with? Did she expect me, a savvy negotiator, to crumble and give in to her initial price? "No thank you," I said. Defiantly, I turned and walked away at a leisurely pace. Surely, she would come running after me. She had poked the bear's pride, and I wouldn't relent. If I had to freeze in these fifty-degree daytime temperatures, that would be better than kowtowing to this over-eager entrepreneur's unreasonable demands.

At a little village called Puerto Ocopa, we settled in for the night. Their sparse, thatched-roof hut provided only a small amount of protection from plunging temperatures. The air grew much colder than I remembered for the jungle, and our

## El Friaje (Without a Jacket)

hosts had no blankets to offer. The only clothing I'd packed included a t-shirt and a pair of shorts.

When we awoke in the morning, my breath hovered in gaseous form. The cold and rainy day promised substantial misery on the river. Our boat sported two motors, a good thing. Bad for me in my barely clothed state, the extra power resulted in faster than normal cruising speeds. The wind ripped across my soon-to-be hypothermic body. I felt the coldest ever in my life. By the time we got to Atalaya, my skeletal system seemed as stiff as a board. My muscles balked when I tried to stand up, and my whole torso shook.

"My friends, I must buy a jacket, or you will bury a corpse on this mission trip," I told my Peruvian friends, half-joking and melodramatic as a soap-opera actor.

We didn't need to walk far before I saw a little market on the main street. A clothing vendor sat quietly near the thoroughfare. Just a few steps further, I stopped. There it is! I spotted almost the same jacket I had seen earlier in the trip. I walked up to the street vendor and casually said, "How much is that one?"

She looked up at me and said in Spanish, "It's sixty-five soles." The price, more than double what I would have paid to the high-jungle vendor, sounded just fine in my freezing condition.

"Sold," I proclaimed, having learned my lesson. Our pride sometimes makes us suffer in more ways than one. It's better to be warm and humble than proud and freezing to death. Even with the jacket, the whole trip included colder-than-normal temperatures. We did not take a bath for three days.

### *Motivation and Money*

Although I am a flawed servant of God, He filled my heart with love for people in these remote areas. I had an almost overwhelming desire to connect with the pastors of each tiny church. Though they might have only ten members, these little outposts of the gospel called to the deep recesses of my heart. Their lives seemed so simple. Any kind of encouragement I brought to these Christians proved well worth the inconveniences to get there. I saw simple faith in action and great trust in the Lord, which encouraged me in return. The native people had nothing by the world's economy. They lived with just the bare essentials, but their commitment to Christ shone like jewels in the Amazon.

Sometimes, as missionaries, our financial support would fluctuate from month to month. We depended on special, end-of-the-year offerings from the United States. Christians seeking tax deductions or realizing their giving had lagged behind their commitment for the year would donate generously in December.

Emma and I waited with excitement for the January report of donations. This became a late Christmas gift for us. The extra donation money provided long-deferred family items or paid off any lingering bills. It brought encouragement to us, like an annual bonus from an employer.

One of the last years of our ministry in Peru, we sat down together and opened our January report. To our surprise, the papers recorded offerings at an all-time monthly low. Not just for January, this became the smallest monthly stipend we ever tried to live on. It caused us to pause, turn to God, and seek His guidance with all our hearts. It became an opportunity to renew our trust in His provision. In the short run, I have to admit that I gave in to some anxiety about finances.

*Ashaninka Soup*

Reeling from the lower donation amount, I still needed to take a planned trip to a village of the Ashaninka tribe. After grumpily traveling the long distance, a friend from Lima and I joined one of the local brothers as guests in his hut.

His thatched-roof structure included only a single room. Exterior walls, made of bamboo, provided a modicum of protection from the elements. The dirt floor contrasted with the nice home Emma and I shared with our children back in the capital city.

Our host invited my friend and me to sit down on a little bench. one of the few pieces of furniture in the hut. We obliged and took our seats. The man's wife and children sat on a little, woven mat next to the fire where she had just cooked our lunch. She rose and served each of us a bowl of soup.

"God in heaven," our host prayed. "Thank you for our friends who came to visit. Thank you for coming with me on my hunting trip last night. Thanks for helping me to kill an armadillo early this morning so we would have good food to serve these men."

His blessing touched my soul and washed away all of my ingratitude for the smaller-than-normal donations in the January report. With tears in my eyes, I looked around the hut with a new appreciation of my host's world. Who am I to argue with God about our support level? It humbled me to see how content and connected to the Lord these people seemed. After his prayer, we all consumed our soup with a new joy in our hearts. Powered by our thankfulness, the way home to Lima seemed much shorter than our trip out to the Ashaninkas.

# 10

## Miracles Sustained Us

On the mission field, it sure seems like God provides more miracles than in ordinary life. Perhaps that's because we need them so often. When trying to accomplish things for God in a new country, lots of things go wrong. I witnessed miracles, some big and some small. They all showed God's loving care throughout the dangers and trials of the missionary life. One of my favorite miracle stories involves a church group who visited Peru from South Carolina.

This high-spirited group came first to Lima, then we all headed to Tarapoto for an outreach campaign. Fifteen people journeyed from the church in South Carolina. A good-natured

Puerto Rican brother led their delegation. Edwin Lugo once won the kick-boxing championship in his weight class at his island homeland. Now he served the Lord by leading this team from their church. His flawless Spanish made him priceless on the mission field, and his endless enthusiasm kept his team's morale high.

A typical day in Tarapoto included evangelistic outreaches to public schools during the day and church services at night. People from Tarapoto have a reputation for their loving nature and their sense of humor. We enjoyed our time with them and laughed more than I had for quite a while.

Tarapoto is in the Northern Amazon. Although in the high jungle, the town is as oppressively hot as many places I visited in the low jungle. Despite the heat and a heavy ministry schedule, all of us seemed to have a blast. The good feelings blossomed as the outreach grew very successful. Many gave their hearts to the Lord or experienced healing for various kinds of physical and mental issues.

After three days of activities, this energetic group wanted a final hurrah. We had one more day and wanted a fun excursion. Our hosts suggested a picturesque waterfall on the outskirts of town, so the team rented two vans and hired drivers. Our plans seemed all set. Then, Edwin had a fateful idea.

"David, is there a chance I might rent a motorcycle to use for this day trip?" he asked. If he had been a blue-eyed gringo, the risky motorcycle ride may have proven too dangerous. The mountainous terrain, the rough, muddy roads, and the sometimes-erratic local drivers might be too much for someone accustomed to highway driving conditions in the United States. Also, a white guy on a motorcycle in this remote area might attract unwanted attention. But, since Edwin looks and acts like a Latino, I gave in to his request ... against my better judgment.

"Edwin, if you are sure you can ride a motorcycle here, I

will try to find you one."

"Oh yes, I rode them all the time back in Puerto Rico, and I would love to get back on one," Edwin assured me.

I inquired of our host church officials to see what they suggested. One of their parishioners not only owned a motorcycle but agreed to lend it to the man of God for a refreshing trip to the waterfall. We seemed all set.

The two vans headed out toward the waterfall with Edwin leading the way on his borrowed motorcycle. We took winding roads over hill and dale, seeking the gorgeous, watery retreat. Once there, our expectations paled in comparison to the Lord's artwork. Lush plants surrounded the idyllic waterfall, cascading into a secluded cove. The miniature paradise took our breath away. We enjoyed dips in the pool beneath the clear, falling water, and the team members even had praise and worship time there. The setting refreshed us and eased our minds.

After two-hours, we loaded ourselves back into the vans and headed toward town. Edwin again led the way on the motorcycle. The beautiful afternoon weather and breath-taking terrain seemed almost divine. As we descended the last mountain, the dirt road narrowed and wound around natural contours of the topography.

I noticed something troubling about the way Edwin took the corners. He negotiated the sharp turns by going left of center. With each bend in the road, he cut into the space that other drivers would need if they approached on the left side of the road. With the washboard texture of the roadway and his substantial speed, I wondered if Edwin might lose control. In the van, I had no way to communicate with him. An ominous feeling swept over me. Desperate, I wanted to yell at Edwin to slow down, to stay in his own lane. As if not complicated enough, Edwin did not wear a helmet.

In a moment, just as we rounded a turn, I saw a taxi coming

the other way. My horror realized, Edwin had no time to react. The cab came barreling into the motorcycle. Edwin slammed into the taxi head-on, ejecting our friend several feet into the air. As if in slow motion, Edwin flew over top of the taxi. His motorcycle impacted the cab's grill, emitting a horrible crunching sound as it bounced off. Like a grainy movie in my mind, Edwin catapulted and did a few somersaults in the air before landing with a crumpled thud on the dirt road. My first thought: Edwin is dead.

Deep pain penetrated my being. How could this happen amid an otherwise perfect week? What would I tell his wife and children?

After a few seconds and quite to my surprise, Edwin leaped to his feet and walked toward us. White as a sheet, his nose bled and looked broken. He waved a dangling thumb at us. I considered passing out, but the pavement outside the van looked hard. Edwin's twisted and broken digit pointed in altogether the wrong direction. It hurt just to look at him.

"I knew I had to get up and walk out of the roadway, or I would die," Edwin said. Although not clear, I think Edwin worried other cars might run him down if he lay in the roadway. However, everyone stopped right away at the sight of the scary-looking accident scene.

"We have to get you to a hospital," I said, trying to keep as calm as possible.

Edwin nodded in agreement as he climbed into the van. After talking among ourselves, we agreed not to wait for an ambulance this far up the mountain. We made Edwin as comfortable as possible and headed down the mountain to the hospital.

"You go. I will stay here and deal with the police and the other driver," offered one of the assistant pastors from our host church.

Fifty-six-year-old Edwin looked bad as we rushed him into

Tarapoto. His coloring went from pale to ashen. My mind raced around all the possibilities. Would I need to stay with him at the hospital for weeks of recovery? Did he have severe and unseen internal injuries? Our team had tickets to fly back to Lima later that evening. Should I change the tickets for Edwin and me? I would stay behind with Edwin, but what about the others? How would they react to the situation?

At the hospital, I called Emma to request urgent prayer. "Honey, there's been a terrible accident. Edwin got hit while riding a motorcycle. Please call everyone we know to ask for prayer."

She agreed and hung up the phone after getting a few details. Just as I hung up the phone, hallelujahs rang out from the emergency room. People clapped and shouted, "Praise God!" The sounds came right from the bay where Edwin lay. What happened?

As soon as I walked into the curtained area, Edwin smiled up at me and said, "Look at my thumb."

My eyes took it all in with difficulty. Once broken and dislocated, his thumb had returned to its normal appearance. There he sat, wiggling his now-healed thumb in my direction. "It's a miracle, David! I am healed!" By every sign, God got busy healing Edwin's thumb while I occupied myself organizing a prayer chain in the next room. As usual, our Lord zoomed way ahead of me.

The nurses dressed Edwin's broken nose and soon sent him on his way. Elation does not describe our emotions. We rejoiced at God's kindness to Edwin and to all of us. He could have died or suffered life-altering injuries. Instead, he flew back to Lima that evening as planned. He reported no more symptoms, except for a big cut on his nose and soreness the next day. I hoped the parishioner's motorcycle insurance covered the accident.

After returning to Lima and resting overnight, Edwin flew

back to Columbia, South Carolina with his church mates. In years to come, we visited his home church often and always laughed about that day when he flew off his borrowed motorcycle. He had one of the shortest broken thumb recoveries on record. This incident reminded me that living for Jesus on the mission field includes many exciting moments, most of them unplanned.

*Daddy/Daughter Date Bombing*
In 2002, Emma heard about the daddy/daughter date concept that later became quite popular in the United States and beyond. She decided I needed to spend quality time with each of our daughters, by themselves, once a month. I agreed. We planned mini-dates with one daughter, then the other. Usually simple, the emphasis went on spending time focusing on my children.

Our home sat within easy walking distance of a shopping mall, about one-and-a-half blocks away. Across the street, the U.S. Embassy stood stoically and reminded me of home. Since Mary liked McDonald's, she picked it for our special time that month. We ordered our favorite sandwiches and their delicious French fries. As we ate and talked, we sat looking at the embassy. The large, stone structure resembled a fortress, rebuilt and fortified following a 1990 bombing there. By 2002, the structure had the reputation that it could even withstand a missile attack. Its impenetrability and stately appearance crossed my mind more than once as we ate our meals.

Our time at the restaurant flew by as I asked my daughter questions and she answered each one with diligence.

"So, Mary, what do you think you'd like to be when you grow up?"

She pondered, then said "I want to be a maid or a newspaper reporter. They both make good money, you know."

I smiled at her innocent exuberance. We talked about many topics of interest to her eight-year-old mind. When we'd finished our meal and exhausted my questions for this visit, we browsed in a bookstore nearby. Both of us loved that store because of the large selection and pleasant atmosphere. We lingered in the children's book section and laughed about some of the books. Finally, we took the short walk home, smiling and chatting along the way. It turned out to be a successful daddy-daughter date.

Soon after we arrived home, Mary filled Emma in on our activities and our discussion. She laughed and smiled while telling Mom about the fun we'd had. Before she even finished her stories, a tremendous explosion shook our building and rattled the windows. Panic gripped us for a few seconds as we tried to process what happened.

"This is bad," I told Emma. "This seems very bad." Hearing an occasional pop or crash seemed normal in the South American city. Even earthquakes shook our building relatively often. But our upscale neighborhood seldom rattled with disturbances of this magnitude. The loud sound and violent shaking definitely felt abnormal.

I hurried to the window to see a plume of black smoke billowing up from the direction of the shopping mall. The news interrupted regular programs, reporting a car bomb exploded right where Mary and I had socialized, just minutes before. The Shining Path terrorists, though declining in power, attempted to make a big splash. Their aim had been to disrupt or cause cancellation of a visit planned later in the week by U.S. President George W. Bush. His visit would include a stop at the embassy.

The bomb did not damage the U.S. embassy, but blew off facades of several storefronts at the mall. The bookstore where Mary and I browsed minutes earlier took heavy damage. Nine or ten people died on the street and in the mall where we strolled only a short time earlier. The bookstore suffered the most physical damage in the attack.

Following the blast, Peruvian President Alejandro Toledo cut short his participation at a U.N. summit in Mexico. President Bush refused to be intimidated and kept his promise to come to Lima a few days later. He paid his respects at a special ceremony to recognize the lives lost. He also met with President Toledo, unmoved by the violence.

Me. Not so much. The bombing episode made me think about the risks my family took each day. I will put my life in danger for the gospel, but I am less sure about putting my family in peril. Several days passed before I calmed down and felt safe again.

For months the bombing haunted me. Just minutes earlier, Mary and I walked by the car that exploded and killed those people. My precious daughter.

*Heavenly Dogs*

In Lima, a city of nine million people, there lurks plenty of danger. Letting our children go anywhere without Emma or me took a substantial act of faith. We love our babies more than we love ourselves. One Saturday evening, Angela and Mary wanted to go to a youth group about an hour away. We knew the church people well, and the youth group had grown large. Since we did not own a vehicle, public transportation remained the only cost-effective option for our missionary family on a tight budget. We trusted our kids and knew the bus ride and the church as safe places for them. At one point, we set aside our fears and agreed to let them go by themselves to the youth group meeting.

Instead of full-size buses, the proprietors used many large vans. They might pack fifteen to twenty people inside each van, which the city must have found more economical to run than large buses. After the girls had navigated on their own to the high school youth group several times without incident, Emma and I became a little more comfortable with these trips across town. The youth group met at their school and most of the participants were also their classmates through the week.

Late one Saturday night, their meeting dismissed, and the girls began their journey home. In Lima at that time, the driver and a co-driver or cobrador had authority to change a route or even decide when to shut the van down for the night. That's what happened as the driver suddenly announced that his vehicle was going out of service. The girls tried to protest, but the driver had authority to stop wherever he wanted.

"This is not our usual spot," Angela pleaded with the driver in Spanish.

"Sorry, this is the end of the line," the driver replied in Spanish. "I am now out of service. Please collect your belongings and exit the van."

The girls complied, knowing they had no other choice. Stepping out into the darkness, they faced an eerie walk the rest of the way home. The girls started walking and praying for God's protection. They spoke softly to each other, encouraging bravery and trust in the Lord.

Out of nowhere, two large dogs approached them. Angela talked to both animals and petted them. When the girls walked, the canines stayed right with them, escorting my daughters as they traveled. Unlike many street dogs that roamed the city, these pooches seemed clean and well behaved. The girls talked to them and petted them, invoking much tail wagging and an occasional bark. As they walked, the dogs stayed right in step.

Before long, Angela recognized a street name, and they turned toward home. Smiling, they continued on their way with their canine escorts. Those two dogs brought great comfort. Once at the door of our apartment building, the girls hugged the dogs goodbye. The pooches wagged their tails and barked a friendly farewell.

As they retold the story to Emma and me, we knew God sent His heavenly canine guards to protect our precious daughters and guide them home safely to us.

The dog escort caper was not to be the only dangerous situation that my family ran into during our time in Lima. On another occasion, Emma and Joshua walked near a popular shopping area. After picking up several items at local shops, they stood on a corner, waiting for a light to change.

Joshua yelled, "Mom, run!"

He and Emma took off down the block, moving as fast as their feet would carry them. First one block, then two, they ran for their lives. When a safe distance away, Joshua stopped and looked back.

"What happened?" Emma asked, still panting.

"Two men with guns approached that blue car near the intersection where we stood. They ordered the driver out of the car. It looked like a car-jacking. They waved guns around. What if a stray bullet came our way?"

Emma and Joshua hurried home, not waiting to get more details. They praised God for His protection as they scampered away from the scene.

### *"I'll Fill You Full of Lead"*

Although we ran into some scary situations, Emma never gave into the fear. She'd lived in Lima for years, first at Bible school, and then with our little family. One evening she told me about an encounter from earlier in the day.

"I was walking down the street distracted with my thoughts, praising and focusing on the Lord," she said. "The day seemed ideal. As I passed the bakery, a man came up beside me and said gruffly, 'I will fill you full of lead.' He intended to rob me. I looked straight into his eyes, and with authority said,

'I rebuke you in the name of Jesus.' Stunned, he stopped following me and just stood there on the sidewalk. Before long, our doorman greeted me as I arrived home."

"Wow. You are one brave lady," I said.

Together safe in our apartment, Emma realized the danger she faced. The full impact of the situation hit her. She trembled a little, and I moved to hold her. We embraced for a long time.

*Mary Gets Lost*
As the children grew older, they became more adventurous and went out on their own more. Joshua and Angela always paid close attention to their circumstances. They easily remembered which bus took them where. Mary, on the other hand, did not pay as much attention because she often traveled with at least one of her older siblings.

Emma tried to tell her, "You need to know for yourself which bus will take you home. What if I'm not with you?"

Mary's reply remained the same. "I know. I know."

One Saturday night, Angela had been ill and did not go to youth group. Mary wanted to spread her new teenage wings and go by herself. Everything went well as she made it to youth group and enjoyed the hours there. When time came for her to board a bus home, Emma and I kept watch on the clock in the dining room. Truthfully, we felt concerned about our youngest out alone at night.

Unbeknown to her and us, Mary boarded the wrong bus coming home. Unlike the time when she and Angela got on the wrong van, she now owned a cell phone. We had given Mary one of ours to take with her for the evening, just in case.

As Emma and I sat at the table, our phone rang in the kitchen.

"Daddy, I do not understand where I am," Mary said in a frightened voice. Only thirteen or fourteen years old, she found herself out on the streets by herself. Vulnerable, she whimpered into the other end of the phone.

I mustered my calm voice. "Tell me honey, do you see a taxi anywhere around you?"

After a moment or two, she managed to compose herself and spotted a taxi heading her way from two blocks in the distance.

"Step off the curb just a little and wave your arms at the taxi," I said.

The driver saw Mary and stopped to pick her up. I stayed on the line with her until she pulled up in front of our house. After paying the driver, I hugged her tight. The bus had only gone a few blocks off her regular route, but the switch was enough of a change to disorient Mary. A few years older, and she may have figured out how to hike the few extra blocks to the right route and catch the correct bus.

*Earthquakes*
Because of its proximity to the Ring of Fire, Peru suffers more than its fair share of earthquakes. After moving to Lima, we stopped noticing quakes below a certain strength during the day. However, we often noticed tremors in the quiet of the night as we lay in bed. Before sensing any movement, there usually came a wall of sound like a large truck barreling up the street.

Right at the foot of the Andes Mountains, I experienced one major earthquake and several smaller ones in our early years in Peru. I began to know when one became imminent.

One day, a friend and I took a van to the airport to meet friends as they arrived for a visit. Along the way, I noticed a tree whipping back and forth beside the road. My brain tried to process what I saw and interpret it. With no wind, I could only think, That's weird.

Next, our van swayed back and forth. Traffic at that hour

can be horrendous and cars surrounded us. While stopped at a traffic light, the earthquake began rocking us more vigorously. Cars blocked us in, so taking evasive action was not an option.

"The van will tip over!" our driver shouted, panic in his voice.

Some people in front of us climbed out of their cars and ran for cover or for open spaces, depending on their level of earthquake knowledge. Our van did not tip over. When it stopped rocking from side to side, we looked around at one another.

Turning to my friend traveling with me, I said, "What a large earthquake! This is way worse than normal!" Eventually, the traffic light turned green, and we continued to the airport. Cell service ceased after the quake and did not soon return, due to infrastructure damage and the surge in calls as people tried to check on their loved ones.

When we rounded the airport access road, we saw damage to the terminal building. Large groups of people had evacuated from the buildings and were milling around outside. We soon learned the earthquake measured 8.0 on the Richter scale, the third-worst in the recorded history of Peru.

The huge columns holding up the portico cracked, reflecting heavy damage. As we got out and peered through the terminal's windows, we saw that significant parts of the ceiling lay in clumps on the floor. Because of the evacuation, customs and immigration activities stopped for a time. Police and customs officials ran around, trying to round up foreign passengers and figure out how to do the required immigration checks outside on the driveway. Airline officials scurried around too, trying to determine how to get bags from planes to the people now standing outside in the parking lot.

After considerable effort, we found our friends and explained about the severity of the earthquake. They knew something significant had happened. With little information, they waited and prayed until we arrived. It took quite a while to retrieve their bags and get them safely home.

One of our pastor friends in Chincha Alta sat in his church alone that day. The entire structure which dated to 1914 came down around him. Miraculously, he emerged unharmed.

All told, a total of 519 people died in Peru because of the 2007 earthquake. The violent shaking had a devastating impact on many people, their homes, and their businesses. Right in Lima proper, our roads suffered only minor damage, but further south in Pisco, Ica and Chincha Alta, 85 percent of the homes sustained damage or complete destruction.

Thankful to get back to our home that evening, my guests and I filled Emma in on the adventure. Unharmed, she and the kids waited for us. They also described the sights and sounds of the earthquake with vivid detail. They were unnerved by the pot lids shaking loudly on the stove in our kitchen. For years after that, Mary would shudder every time she heard a lid shaking as a pot boiled.

# 11

## Flying Under the Radar with Chicken Campero

As a missionary, I often had to fly from one place to another. One of the best flights back to the United States routed me through El Salvador. Besides the cheaper price, this route divided the flight time almost evenly: a four-hour flight from Peru to El Salvador and a second four-hour leg to Washington, D.C. Being an astute observer, I quickly noticed something strange when going through customs at Dulles. Some of my fellow travelers carried box lunches that smelled like heaven.

"How is it that these people get to bring in chicken boxed lunches, but you confiscate even a small piece of fruit from me?" I asked a customs official.

"Well, cooked chicken is not subject to seizure," the man replied pleasantly. "Fruit might contain pests that escape into the air and spread from one country to another."

It's hard to explain what emotions the aroma of that chicken evoked. Perhaps the long travel time and cramped conditions affected my senses, but I deeply desired to get some of that chicken. My heart and soul longed for a pollo dinner in ways only a true chow hound understands. Little did I know the clandestine operation involved in buying chicken Campero in Central America.

The next time I flew through El Salvador, my resolve must have registered through the roof. I am always game for something new, but this chicken had captured my full attention. Behind the security checkpoint at San Salvador, I spied no pollo places. I walked up and down through the terminal twice, but I found no satisfaction.

Undaunted, obsessed even, I approached a tall guard with a serious expression. The name on his uniform read Ramirez.

"I smell this wonderful chicken, but how do I get some for my trip?" I asked with a sly wink.

As if describing a top-secret procedure, the guard pulled me close. He subtly pointed, then said in hushed tones, "You go to that phone over there. You call this number, then you walk to the scanners by the security checkpoint. A man will deliver the chicken to you." He handed me a small piece of paper with the phone number of the pollo joint. For emphasis, he added, all very James Bond-like, "You must pay in cash."

A little skeptical and mildly suspicious, I dialed the cloak-and-dagger digits.

In Spanish, I spoke in a low voice. "I'm in the airport and would like chicken Campero delivered."

Someone grunted in reply. Not sure if I had dialed the right number or perhaps missed a secret password, I waited anxiously for more of a response, which came after a pregnant pause.

"Yes." A mysterious female voice purred into the other end of our connection. "How many dinners do you desire?"

I ordered two whole chickens, intending to bring this precious quarry back to the States to share with family. After waiting only a few minutes, I strolled to the security checkpoint and stood by, hoping and dreaming about that intoxicating meal.

Soon, a guard approached boldly and challenged me, "Sir, what are you doing?"

"I am waiting for some chicken," I said nonchalantly. The guard nodded knowingly and walked back to his post with military precision. As he stood back at his post, his face showed a level of compassion that approached spiritual understanding. Pollo so delicious disrupts life. This chicken business transcended borders, security concerns, and everything else. In a few minutes, the delivery guy showed up on the other side of the checkpoint. He handed my food over the top of the scanner, in full view of the guards. The delivery man took my cash payment and his tip. Then he was gone.

I paused, thinking what nefarious contraband traveled through the airport disguised as takeout meals. At that moment, it didn't matter. After happily collecting my booty, I headed straight to the gate and my flight. Safely on the plane, the chicken and I peacefully coexisted for four hours until we touched down in familiar territory.

As I negotiated the U.S. customs area at Dulles, my Salvadoran chicken dinner received the same reverence as similar meals I had smelled on previous trips. No one asked about my Styrofoam container or offered to peek inside. Later that night, my host family and I dined on Pollo Campero for supper. Reheated, the chicken filled the house with a heavenly aroma and tasted just as good as the fragrant emanation I remembered.

*Fleas on a Plane*

In our hunt for economical airfare, I found a Lima travel agent who gave us the most amazing deals. Although at the time unsure of his methods, we later learned that Roberto served the Catholic Church as one of their primary Peruvian travel agents. Catholic clergy is exempt from taxes on anything in Peru. Therefore, the tickets intended for clergy had markings to show the special status. My tickets bore this marking familiar to the airline gate personnel.

At one point, I began to notice strange looks from airport officials whenever I flew with my wife and three children. Once I understood more about our tickets, I put two and two together. Perhaps they imagined me a wayward Catholic priest, instead of the upstanding non-denominational minister and family guy that I am.

Roberto would not get us the most convenient flights, but always by far the cheapest. One flight on a Venezuelan airline took us through Caracas. With Hugo Chavez as dictator of Venezuela, their government occasionally showed anti-American sentiments. On this trip, I packed a bunch of books, printed in Peru, for distribution in the U.S. My family and I headed through security in Caracas, not realizing that our suitcases would be x-rayed, as we made our way through the airport to our gate.

Once seated on the plane, the flight attendant called my name. "David Bredeman, please come to the front of the plane, por favor."

My wife and children looked on with apprehension as I rose and made my way to the front. I walked calmly through the plane to the jetway, where I came upon a stern-looking Venezuelan official.

# Flying Under the Radar with Chicken Campero

The official and another uniformed man seemed nervous. The older of the two asked me to deplane and follow them. We walked down an exterior staircase next to the jetway. I climbed into a golf cart with the government officials, and we rolled off with a whir. Eventually, the golf cart turned and entered a warehouse, still on airport grounds. While I stood nearby, one of the uniformed men opened my luggage and looked at the books. Apparently, the x-rays of the books looked like bundles of cocaine, something frequently smuggled out of Peru. When it turned out to be "just books," the official seemed surprised and disappointed. After some disapproving looks and a tsk tsk or two, they drove me back to the plane.

When we landed in the U.S., I anxiously opened my suitcase to find all the books still in there. Unfortunately, my sunglasses and cell phone had disappeared. For the rest of the trip, I squinted a lot and frequently asked Emma for time checks. Fortunately, I easily picked up a replacement cell phone.

On our return flights, we again passed through Caracas. My son Joshua, being a joker, pointed out through the window of the plane. "Look Dad, we probably will see that same government guy talking on your cell phone and wearing your sunglasses."

I smiled at his burgeoning since of humor.

During these episodes, we questioned the value of our bargain flights. I lost a phone and my sunglasses. When Josh got home, we realized he had been bitten by fleas while on the plane. Unfortunately, that was not the last time we economized using that same travel agent. We needed the bargain flights, fleas or no fleas.

### *Miami Robbery*
On one of our "Roberto bargain" trips, flight times required

us to overnight in Miami. The sleazy hotel Roberto booked for us looked like something from a bad detective movie. As the airport shuttle let us out, we reluctantly carried everything we'd brought with us into the minimalist hotel lobby. I stacked the bags around Emma and the kids, then headed over to the desk to check all of us into our rooms. They had our reservations, and everything seemed in order.

When I came back from the front desk just a few feet away, I asked Emma, "Where's my briefcase?"

She looked around, then gestured that she did not know.

A guy sitting in the corner said, "A man just came through here. He picked up a briefcase and continued out the door."

I raced to the door and looked out. Seeing no one, I walked back to Emma.

"Oh honey, I am so sorry," Emma said.

"I'm a dummy," I replied. "I should have kept my case with me." It had so much in there: eight passports (since each of our three kids had dual citizenship at the time); Emma's green card; and my calendar portfolio with all my scheduled appointments and speaking engagements for the next two months. I had also brought along some counterfeit Peruvian money I planned to use as a visual aid for my missionary sermons.

How could I have left my briefcase in such a vulnerable place? Emma and the kids expressed regret they let the briefcase get stolen, but I didn't blame them. We called the police. They came to the hotel to take a report but offered little hope of getting our things back.

"It's probably lying outside a crack house somewhere," said the hard-boiled policeman.

Along with all the other things in the briefcase, we lost the plane tickets for our flight, scheduled to take us to Washington the next day. I called the airline and threw myself on their mercy.

"No problem, sir," the voice on the phone assured me. "Just show up at the airport early. You can fly as if you still had the tickets in hand."

This minor tragedy fell right at the time when airlines transitioned from paper tickets to paperless tickets. Unfortunately, I had the paper kind. The next morning, we strode to the ticket counter and repeated the story and the promises of the person on the phone.

The lady behind the ticket counter said to Emma, "I am sorry, ma'am. We will have to re-print your tickets and charge you $100 per person for a change fee from paper to e-tickets."

I explained that the re-ticketing fee would be a problem for us. We then stepped away from the desk.

"Hold on, Emma. Let me check into renting a van." I walked to the nearest rental car company and asked about renting a van big enough for our family of five, plus luggage. The van would have been $600 plus gasoline for one-way and to drop the car in Virginia.

We headed back to the airline desk, and I asked to speak with a manager, praying all the way.

"Sir, our tickets and several other things were stolen from us at our motel," I pleaded. "We can't pay extra fees."

"I am sorry, it will cost you $100 apiece," he said, his voice void of mercy. "That's our policy for paper tickets."

"But sir, we don't have $500," I said.

"Oh, there are more of you? More than just the two of you?"

"Yes, we have our three kids with us." I motioned to the three of them sitting pitifully in the corner with dejected looks on their faces.

"Give them the tickets," the manager told an agent nearby.

We flew back to Washington still aching about losing all our documentation. I felt beside myself about losing the passports, envisioning the laborious task of standing in line for eight passports and visas again. Plus, we would need to replace Emma's U.S. green card. Sorting all this out might easily occupy our whole time in the U.S. Per Emma, my dejected expression lasted the entire flight.

Two days later, we sat in my mother's living room when the phone rang. My mother answered, then she motioned excitedly for me.

"It's for you, David. It's someone from the State Department."

I greeted the man on the line and verified my identity.

"Mr. Bredeman, we've found all of your passports."

"How can this be?" I asked.

"A police officer in Miami found them in a trashcan."

Truly a miracle, we got back all eight passports and Emma's green card. The documents included everything except for the counterfeit Peruvian money. The State Department mailed the contents back to us from Miami.

"Your tax dollars at work," I proudly said to my mother. "Thank you, State Department."

"Thank you, Lord! Such a relief!" Mother replied.

# 12

## Hunting the Mashco-Piros

One seminal trip changed the focus of our ministry in Peru. The Mashco-Piros tribe is one of the last uncontacted people groups in Peru. They are hard to locate because they move around nomadically. After hunting and fishing in one area, the tribe moves on. Once they've caught or scared off most of the wildlife, they move again. Since they live in rudimentary huts formed from leaves, their residences biodegrade quickly and are difficult to detect just two weeks after the tribe vacates them.

While on a visit to the States, I spoke with a specialist from Florence, South Carolina about risks associated with meeting the Mashco-Piros. Dr. Peter Johnson, a renowned expert on contacting indigenous peoples, told me I would have a 50 percent chance of surviving—if we found the Mashco-Piros. He told me that the tribe might fill us full of arrows just out of fear. Dr. Johnson's organization, New Tribes Mission, had learned much by studying the process of reaching primitive tribes. He'd seen and studied countless interactions. Often, remote people fear for their own lives and those of their wives and children. Because of recent or even ancient experiences, they fear outsiders might steal their family members and carry them far away.

The Mashco-Piros remained on my heart for ten of my fifteen years in Peru. Some ministry friends in the small city of Cuzco said they would help me search. We traveled first to Madre de Dios, arranging a thirty-five-foot boat and buying fifty-five-gallon drums of gasoline. The search could take at least one week to travel through the lower jungle and then a week to return home.

Once outfitted, our team traveled upriver, excited by what we might find. Our guide, Octavio, brought years of experience. My trust in him grew because I had seen his expertise on a previous journey.

Of the ten persons on our team. I was the only non-Peruvian. As a group, we spoke three different native languages. We hoped that when we found the Mashco-Piros, someone on our team could communicate with them. Several of the tribes in this region speak similar tongues. After several years in the country, I learned about using common ground to build alliances. Quechua, Piro, and Shipibo are three important language groups of the indigenous people. Some also speak Spanish.

For the first part of our journey, we followed the Los Amigos river, a tributary to the Amazon. We chose the month of August and this specific route because August is when river turtles go ashore to lay eggs. If our plan worked, we would find the Mashco-Piros coming out of the forest to harvest turtle eggs on the river's sandy beaches. Knowledge of this habit served as our best intel on how to find them. We hoped to make friendly contact in a remote area of the Amazon jungle.

In August, the rainfall stops over much of the Peruvian lower jungle. Our thirty-five-foot dugout canoe, laden with supplies and gasoline, experienced difficulty getting up the shrinking river. Many times, we ran aground. The only option available to us, we climbed out of the boat and pushed until it floated again. These forays out of the boat held many dangers because the depth of the river changed dramatically. We also dodged snakes, caimans, and piranhas in the muddy waters.

Once out of the boat, we pushed the craft until we reached knee-deep water depth. Getting moving again, we switched from men pushing to peque-peque motor to regular boat motor. The process proved slow and frustrating. In the evenings, we camped on sand bars or beaches and bathed in the river. Only one woman came with us. She and her husband hailed from the Shipibo tribe, and she served as our cook. Most of our meals came from canned tuna and rice, cooked over the campfire.

The sandy river bottom was not the only hazard. Our guides helped us dodge trees floating in the river and lodged on sandbars. Even large vines can snag the boats. In other places, the current washed away the sand and carved deep pockets in the water. A sudden drop off, with the water becoming deep, created dangerous holes where people had lost their lives.

Bug repellent did not work because it washed off every time we got in the water. At one point, I became covered in bug bites from my knees to my feet. The itching weighed heavily on my mind with more than a hundred bites covering my legs. The heat. The muddy river. The itching. I reached a place of total misery. Even with my experience in the jungle, this trip registered in my mind as much more miserable than usual.

In agony, I cried out to God. I told the Lord that the itching had become unbearable and my life had become untenable. My agony reached beyond my human tolerance level. Perhaps the discomfort might force me to give up our search.

"Can you handle just one bug bite at a time?" the Lord asked.

I thought about the question. "Yes, Lord. I can." From that point forward, God opened my mind to experience just one bite at a time with each itch localized to one place on my body. This word of inspiration took away my discomfort, and I stopped worrying about the bugs. What an answer to prayer!

Traveling in the jungle brings the very significant risk of serious infection. The most serious risks come from piranhas, anacondas and caimans. If we experienced a large bite that became infected in the warm, moist climate, we could die before getting back to civilization.

As we traveled upstream, I told our guide what Dr. Johnson had predicted. Our guide did not believe Dr. Johnson's dire assessment.

Octavio patted me on the shoulder. "We don't have a lot to worry about. If we contact the Mashco-Piros, they will be in hunting mode, not war mode. If they are in war mode, they carry twenty arrows apiece. In hunting mode, each warrior carries only three or four arrows. So, you only have to worry about three or four arrows per warrior." I laughed at his gallows humor, but his words stuck in my mind like a pointy arrow.

On this evening, the sun set faster than normal and the river scenery turned dark. A small howler monkey called out our location from high in a nearby tree. The livelihood of the Mashco-Piros depends on hitting small monkeys like that, a target the size of my liver. Marvelous, I thought, only three or four arrows in my liver. Nothing to worry about.

We soon realized we had company. While looking for the Mashco-Piros, signs of illegal loggers turned up instead. Coveted mahogany trees, which comprised their prize quarry, floated on the river like so many calling cards. In the jungle, mahogany trees don't grow in convenient clumps or groves. The loggers find the desired trees hundreds of yards apart. After cutting them down, the loggers lash the trees together into rafts and float them downstream to market. Besides the other dangers on the river, we also passed loggers sitting on rafts made of mahogany logs.

Where one found loggers, one would not find many animals. Their noise and destruction drove the animals away. The logging men posed a danger for the Mashco-Piros in several ways. This meant the two groups avoid one another. We soldiered on anyway, looking for sandy areas where the turtles might lay eggs. The further upstream we got, the more often we had to get out of the boat and push the sizable watercraft.

If we spotted any clearing near a sandy shore, we would park the boat and check for signs of the Mashco-Piros. Footprints and certain types of arrows provide a clue to their location, but the jungle grew thick near the riverbank. Our search continued in futility with no sign of the mysterious tribe.

On the tenth day, after we had pushed the boat more than we floated it, we deemed the time right to turn around and head back home. That last night, before we planned to give up, we followed our normal routine. In the evening time together, our guide and I pitched tents. In almost no time, the Shipibos created a bamboo and leaf structure out of whatever the jungle offered. Sometimes they would have their sleeping space set up before I could erect my one-man tent.

With a fire in the middle of our camp and the sleeping

structures around it, we relished our time together. After dinner, I told Bible stories using special methods I had been taught in missions school. Bible storying provided maximum learning for people with limited formal schooling. These hours represented golden opportunities to share knowledge about God's Word. Our team seemed to enjoy the stories, asking lots of questions. Their challenges stretched me; some of their ideas had never occurred to my Western mind. The teaching/learning process knitted our hearts together, and I grew as a believer and a person.

Caimans sometimes came close to our camp but found our fire off-putting. If the water might be only ten yards from us, we heard a loud symphony of caimans and other wildlife.

Not all the fauna posed a danger to us. This far out, we thrilled to idyllic flocks of parrots, parakeets and macaws. Every so often, a salt lick, or outcropping of mud, allowed a menagerie of wild birds to harvest salt for their diet. The birds mined the salt from the mud while basking in glorious sunshine. The memory of huge walls of brightly colored feathers and the magnificence of parrots in flight still lights up my imagination. These fascinating scenes remain etched deep in my mind. My fondest reminders of the jungle keep me thankful for my missionary years.

Red howler monkeys provided an interesting part of our jungle backdrop. At four in the morning, they might make noises that sounded like a Jurassic Park soundtrack. The first time I heard howler monkeys, I thought What in the world is that? A protrusion from their massive throats looks like a goiter. This anatomical feature facilitates the great volume of their cries.

Near the end of our hunt for Mashco-Piros, as we lay in our tents, a monkey cried out in the jungle. I saw nothing on this clear, moonless night. My soul rested and took in all the magnificent creation around me. As I pondered the magnificence of it all, God sent a reminder of the wildness of our surroundings. With no warning, something large moved around the outskirts of our tents.

"David, do you hear that sound?" Octavio whispered.

"Yes, do you know what's hanging around out there?"

"I'll show you in the morning."

Although not reassured, I trusted Octavio and drifted off to sleep.

When we arose, he pointed out panther tracks all around our campsite. "I guess we did not smell like something the big cat wanted to eat," I said.

"The panther must not have been hungry for gringo," Octavio said, laughing. "And I am too old and tough to eat. Every animal in the jungle knows it."

Before we broke camp on that Sunday morning, we held a little church service. We sang a chorus or two. As we prepared for breakfast, a lone fellow came floating down the river on a mahogany raft. He looked like an older Huck Finn, maybe in his early thirties. He had lighter skin than many of the indigenous people and sported a beard, most unusual for that jungle area. Although we did not expect guests, we invited him over to our camp.

"Hey, would you like breakfast?" I called to him in Spanish. "Our food tastes delicious."

"Yeah, sure," he responded, also in Spanish. "My name is Jose."

The man paddled over and pulled his raft onto our sandbar. It did not take long for us to realize he was starving. He consumed three breakfasts before stopping to talk.

"Tell us a little about yourself, Jose." Octavio said. "What are you doing out here in the jungle?"

"I am going home–back to the city," Jose replied. "I worked at logging in my last job, but they never paid us. After weeks without pay and little food, I refused to take it anymore."

"That isn't right," I said. "They should have paid you."

"I worked hard, and there is a lot of risk," he said. "What brings you out here?"

"We are looking for the Mashco-Piros," I replied. "Have you seen them?"

"Yes," he said. "Not a pleasant experience, but I saw them."

The hair on the back of my neck stood up. "Where?" I asked. "When?"

"That's one reason I left the logging job. We chop down the mahogany trees wherever they grow. Then, a logger foreman cuts the big tree trunk into heavy planks that we men carry out to the river. One man is responsible to tie the planks together and start them down the river. Others collect the rafts and take the wood to market. Anyway, myself and another guy carried a load of heavy planks on our shoulders. As we walked toward the river, two arrows flew across our path. The arrows darted right in front of us. Without a second thought, we threw down our planks and ran for our lives. I got a look at the men that shot at us."

Our guest described the Mashco-Piros, and my companions confirmed the description sounded right.

"I decided right then to quit logging and head for home" Jose said. "I ran to the river, got on a raft, and headed downstream. Someone called after me, but I ignored them."

As we talked to him those few minutes, Jose brought up a strange subject. "Nothing in my life works out right because I am an illegitimate son. This curse follows me everywhere."

To our surprise, he pulled out his birth certificate, which identified his father as Mexican. Bold letters proclaimed: "An Illegitimate Child." Jose Ramirez carried this label with him everywhere in life. We found the situation odd that a man in his thirties continued to live under the cloud of illegitimacy as his primary identity, to the point of bringing it up to strangers after only a few minutes. His birth name, common in this region, would make it easy for him to live in anonymity.

"Jose, I have the most wonderful news for you," I said. "We have a heavenly Father who wants to adopt you. Through the sacrifice of His Son Jesus, you can become a legitimate son of the most-high God right here today."

We looked at the Scripture in Paul's letter to the Galatians: "But when the fullness of the time had come, God sent forth His Son, born of a woman, born under the law, to redeem those who were under the law, that we might receive the adoption as sons. And because you are sons, God has sent forth the Spirit of His Son into your hearts, crying out, 'Abba, Father!' Therefore you are no longer a slave but a son, and if a son, then an heir of God through Christ" (Galatians 4:4-7).

On that sandy river bank, deep in the lower Amazon, Jose gave his heart to Jesus and became a legitimate child of God. His conversion blessed everyone in our group. We experienced God's Spirit moving all around us.

Even though we did not find the Mashco-Piros, Jose made the whole trip worthwhile. Although we searched for an entire tribe of people to evangelize, God took us to a singular young man who needed to exchange his false identity for a true one.

"Jose, after a person accepts Jesus, the Bible suggests some next steps. These things don't save you; Jesus completed that work on the cross. But baptism shows that we have accepted God's gift of salvation and sonship. Will you follow Jesus and show it through getting baptized?"

After thinking for a moment, Jose looked at me and said "David, I want very much to get baptized, but not here. There is a beautiful spot downstream where the Los Amigos River meets the Madre de Dios River. Can you baptize me there?"

"Sure Jose," I agreed. "Let's head down there now."

Jose abandoned his raft and rode with us in our boat. The

slow pace of the river allowed considerable time for talking. I sat with Jose and learned about his work history in the jungle. The treatment he suffered at the hands of his various employers played into his low self-esteem. He worked in each of the three main industries of this jungle region: illegal logging, harvesting of Brazil nuts, and river gold mining. As we rode along, he explained the three jobs in great detail. His tales opened my eyes.

"Brazil nuts grow in round spheres," he said. "They are like walnuts, only bigger, and they have a tough outer shell. When you remove this outer shell, you see the inner wedges encased in their own hard shells. The outer sphere is about the size of a softball. Remember that the trees may grow two hundred feet tall."

"Oh, I know what you will say," I said while grabbing my own skull.

"When the spheres of Brazil nuts fall off the trees, the impact can be lethal. I saw a man die while we picked up Brazil nuts from the ground." He paused, processing the hurt from the memory. "Timing for harvesting is crucial. If you harvest too early, there is considerable danger from the falling nuts. If you come too late, they rot on the jungle floor. Our employers did not give us helmets or anything. That man's death ended my Brazil nut harvesting job."

"Understandable," I said, wiping sweat from my brow and dipping my hand in the muddy river. The noonday sun scorched my skin again. I poured a little water on my neck to cool off.

"With logging, the scout goes out to find a tree. The rest of us waited until he called out to us. Then, we'd make our way through the jungle to him. We cut down each mahogany tree and carried away the planks. By the time we finished with one tree, the scout would have located the next tree and so on. Since the scout searched out ahead of the team, he held

## Hunting the Mashco-Piros

responsibility for hunting. Once all the men showed up, we scared away any animals with our sawing and other noise. Unfortunately, our scout did not excel at hunting. We mainly just starved. He seldom killed any game for us to eat."

"Oh, no," I said. "That's heavy work with no food."

"Can you imagine in this heat, carrying boards, barefoot, to the river? The hard work did not scare me, but we got no pay and no food. What scared me? The Mashco-Piros terrified me. Once we knew they did not chase us, I realized they could have filled us with arrows. They just wanted to scare us away. Before I left, we tried to circle back to our base camp. When we sneaked back there, the Mashco-Piros had destroyed everything. They sent a clear signal they did not want us anywhere around there."

"I think you did the right thing. We saw other loggers on the river, but they told us they'd never seen the Mashco-Piros."

"That's what told us to say. They hope you will turn around and not interfere in the logging business. So far, the government authorities have little control out here. Some politicos probably get a cut of the logging money. We don't know. One thing is for sure, most people don't care about the Mashco-Piros or any of us poor souls that try to make a living out here."

The canoe made steady progress almost hypnotizing us with gentile rocking. We passed water around to each person and Jose again drank a great deal.

"My other bad job in the jungle centered on gold mining. The company guys set up a sluice box right in the river. They sent us men down to vacuum gold from the river bottom. The gold flakes just lay down there, mixed in with sand and stone. Divers get two hoses, a big one for vacuuming and a smaller one for oxygen. We sucked on the oxygen hose and put clothespins on our nose to keep the air from escaping. We wore lead anklets to keep us down on the bottom."

"That sounds scary," I said. "Did you find it as dangerous

as it sounds?"

"Much worse. Sometimes we found a rich spot, and several mining barges would cluster in one place on the river. Divers from several boats dove at the same time. They tried to elbow each other out of the way. I tried to be as careful as possible, but the competition became intense. Without realizing it, you might vacuum yourself into a hole or a cave. If you saw rocks and sand above you, a dangerous cave-in became imminent. If a diver did not react in time, it meant death. Several of my co-workers were buried alive. All that rock and sand just fell in on them."

"That's awful." I hurt, just thinking about the men who lost their lives.

"One day, I was working up top," Jose continued. "Something bad happened to the man down below. We figured he got buried by a cave-in. His air hose floated to the surface. Those animals I worked for did not even send anyone down to search for the man. 'It is too late for him,' they told me. 'Now get down there.' The deaths became rampant, but the company's view: next man up. Mining people die all the time. The river habitat is being damaged too, and no one cares."

After hearing all of Jose's trials trying to make a living, his baptism brought me even more satisfaction and joy. God saved Jose from all those dangers so that Jose might transform into a legitimate son. After the baptism and a little more fellowship, we parted company. As he floated off in a different direction, I hoped I might see this new convert again in this lifetime, but this seemed unlikely.

We never contacted the Mashco-Piros. In retrospect, that may have been for the best. God loves all people, and He has a plan for them too, just as he does for each of us. With their isolated immune system, an ill-timed visit could bring a fatal disease to the Mashco-Piros. Their nomadic lifestyle would make follow-up and further Christian teaching difficult.

Perhaps the right people to bring the gospel to the Mashco-Piros will have a better plan or teaching method than ours.

We spent two weeks in a boat so one person could find his way to Jesus, and that miracle seemed enough for us. It sounded like something Jesus would do.

*Love for Peru*
Perhaps it's my Boy Scout upbringing that caused me to love my time in the Peruvian rain forest. The beauty and excitement became like heaven in my mind. The exotic setting, the potential for danger, the uniqueness of the experiences—all captured my heart. As a teacher, two weeks spent with people who are eager to learn is priceless. Little did I realize how much that trip would affect my future ministry to Peruvians.

As we parted company with Jose and headed for home, we still had a few difficult days remaining on the river. Our designated hunter and husband of the food preparer used the lone shotgun we had. The gun included parts from at least three others, cannibalized over the years and fit together. Components of this weapon might have been a hundred years old.

With his ancient, cobbled-together shotgun, he could get off only one shot at a time. Frequently, the shell lodged in the chamber. When that happened, he used a long stick to clear the jam from the barrel or to remove the spent casing.

His wife served as our spotter. With eyes like an eagle, she saw game long before the rest of us. When she pointed out a potential target, her husband would get excited, grab his shotgun, but forget to take his ramming stick with him. He had to hit the animal on the first shot. If not, his prey would get away while he searched for another stick long enough to clear the barrel. He often missed. Either way, he lived up to his nickname, "One-Shot Wonder."

Most of the time, we ate tuna and rice. After a week and a

half, we'd had only two birds and no game to augment our tuna diet.

"Guide, sir, some monkey might taste good for a change," I suggested.

"We've seen them but have not been able to get a good bead on one," he replied.

As we continued down the river, the going remained hard. With little rain, we jumped out many times to push the boat along. After a long day, we grew eager to find a sandbar to camp for the night. As darkness approached, our search became more urgent, but no landing place appeared. If we did not find a sandy stopping place soon, we might spend a night trying to sleep in the boat. Because of the thickness of the jungle, potential stopping places were scarce. Sand gave protection from insects, snakes and other wildlife.

As the others scanned the river banks for a sandbar, I kept looking up in the trees, hoping to see a monkey. We'd spied one or two, but not where our marksman might get a shot.

"Mono!" I yelled.

Upon hearing the Spanish word for monkey, "One-Shot Wonder" leaped into action. While I had only seen one monkey at first, soon, an entire family of monkeys came into view. Bam, a shot rang out through the jungle, and we heard the heavy sound of dead weight falling through the canopy and the louder thud of our prey making impact on the jungle floor.

Two of the men jumped out of the boat and retrieved the animal. Once they placed the monkey into our boat, the men jumped in, followed by "One-Shot Wonder." As providence would have it, a sandbar appeared just a hundred feet down the river from where the monkey fell.

We made camp in the fading light while our cook prepared the meal. Because of the size of the animal, we supposed the mature monkey must have been the dominant male in the family. As we sat down to eat, the howls of the other monkeys invaded our ears.

"The honored spotter of the monkey gets the first piece of meat," Octavio said. He handed it to me by extending the spit in my direction. I took off a chunk, and he passed the meat to the others.

As the bite neared my mouth, the monkeys mourned loudly the loss of their father, their mate, their brother. Grief welled up in me. "This must be the saddest meal I have ever consumed," I said.

"You are so right," another team member agreed.

"I wish we had eaten tuna again tonight," I said to no one in particular.

The pathetic cries of the monkey family drove home the pain of their loss and haunted my sleep. As I lay there in what had been my sanctuary, I doubted my status as an Amazon warrior.

*New Focus*

The trip in search of the Mashco-Piros opened me to new ideas. Although stories of swashbuckling through the jungle play well with supporters back home, the time I spent teaching and working with those on our search team proved much more fruitful. The gravity of Jose's salvation and the spiritual growth of my traveling companions hit me like a ton of bricks. I was eager to share my thoughts with Emma back in Lima.

In all my travels to the back country, my presence did not appear to be changing lives for the long term. Something different brewed in my spirit: the rumblings which often preceded God turning the ship of my life. Where might it lead? I didn't know yet.

Emma did not say much that first night home. After years as my wife, she knew I needed rest before any big conversations. After a pleasant welcome meal and a long, hot shower, my eyes begged for sleep, and the bed enveloped me. On the night of my return, I slept a solid thirteen hours. On the verge of complete exhaustion, something about returning home gave me the freedom to sleep on a deep level—no panthers trying to eat me or snakes crawling into my bed. Home meant safety.

Emma's patience with this process says much about her Christian maturity and her love for me. After holding the fort alone with the children for two weeks, she knew my first afternoon and night home would involve sleeping and little else.

In the morning, my rested body emerged from our bedroom. Emma cooked breakfast, and we sat holding hands. She'd experienced this post-jungle ritual and knew all the ins and outs of my recovery process, but this time I needed to talk. Not knowing where to jump in, I shared my heart.

"Emma, I had an epiphany during my travels."

"You did?" she said, looking squarely at me.

"We need to change the focus of our ministry."

"I am listening." She poured me a second cup of coffee.

"These long trips into the jungle have not provided the kind of results I've hoped to see. Even at the conferences we've led on the other side of the Andes, the people react well at the moment. Then, I come back six months later, and they are struggling with many of the same issues and problems ... like the teaching isn't sinking in or transforming anyone."

Emma looked into my eyes as if she were taking the temperature of my soul. Maybe she wondered if my tiredness was talking?

"What are you thinking you want to do?" Her smile warmed me.

"We need to concentrate on the ministers who work with these people every week. I am thinking we shift focus to helping the pastors grow, training them, caring for them, and encouraging them. We need to help them stay in the fight. Each time I travel to the remote churches, I find pastors who are hurting. Their energy level seems low. Many appear so burdened with problems and cares from their ministry. I think if we work with them, teaching them better methods of ministry, it might create a much broader impact than doing three-day conferences at their church members."

"I understand," Emma replied. "Would you work with the pastors one-one-one or have teaching conferences here in Lima?"

"Both. Let's organize conferences twice a year at Catedral de Fe. Not all the pastors would come. At least not to every conference, but a good number would. The church pastoral team might provide teaching for the wives too. If needed, I can get outside speakers too. My heart cries out for the couples I've met, beaten down by stress and problems. Perhaps it's time to offer our home as a retreat for short visits. Let's pray and pour ourselves into one couple at a time."

Emma took in all my words and offered her thoughts and observations. That conversation turned our lives around. In the coming weeks and months, we transformed our ministry focus—with the love and support of our home church in Lima.

Results came within days. Couple after couple contacted us and wanted to come for visits. Over the coming months, we saw God move in mighty ways to repair hearts, fix marriages, and energize tired souls. By focusing on the ministry providers, we strengthened the fabric of the clergy in Peru. So far, so good. This ministry began to flourish and expanded for the next four to five years.

*Meanwhile, Back in the U.S.*
I traveled to the United States often to meet with our mission's board and to speak at our sponsoring churches. Losing

touch with sponsors is often the death of missionary funding. Even as I tried to make regular communication with supporters a major goal, our funding levels continued to drop. One of our main sending churches dissolved, cutting $600 per month from our support. With the kids gone, Emma and I made drastic lifestyle changes to survive.

Circumstances forced us to move from the place we had lived our whole time in Peru to a much less safe part of town. We sought the Lord about each financial issue many times, but no clear-cut answers came.

Even as we fought to maintain and to rebuild our support relationships back in the U.S., our ministry in Peru flourished. Our experiences with clergy from distant areas proved rewarding and gave us hope. Emma and I saw great healing and encouragement poured out to these visiting couples. Most of them had little money and could not afford to pay us for the services Emma and I provided. The costs of hosting them had to come out of our shrinking household budget.

*Just a Little Wine for the Stomach's Sake*
The stress of our funding situation and lack of emotional support from back home grew more intense. My mental fatigue manifested itself in health problems, including symptoms of cardiovascular disease. When the discomfort drove me to our family physician, I knew we couldn't afford any expensive form of treatment. The doctor knew nothing of my previous bout with over-drinking, and I didn't tell him when he prescribed a little wine with dinner.

I soon discovered that Peruvian wine tastes fantastic. To think it might also eliminate my stomach problems sounded too good to be true. The memory of my previous alcohol dependence faded and seemed irrelevant. Now fifteen years in the rear view mirror, how could the issue matter now?

My doctor did not have to suggest the treatment twice. If

Emma had reservations, she deferred to the medical professional's better judgment and to my quoting of 1 Timothy 5:23: "Stop drinking only water and use a little wine because of your stomach and your frequent illnesses." Soon, we added wine to the dinner menu.

Because of the changes in our ministry focus, I did not have to travel as much to the churches in the back country. This meant more time with just Emma and me and wine. Visits from clergy continued, but not on any regular schedule. When they visited, I abstained from wine. As soon as they left, wine reappeared in my daily regimen. Just a glass at dinner and an occasional follow-up glass later in the evening.

# 13

## Tipsy in the Spirit

Despite seeing the hand of God working in so many ways, discouragement recurred like an unwanted friend. Unlike most phases of my missionary journey, I found myself unprepared when this final season arrived. It is easy to forget that alcohol is a depressant.

After my accidental call to ministry all those years earlier, I began with lofty visions of the missionary life. The wonder of God's provision, the beauty of my adopted country, and the gentleness of the Peruvian people fulfilled many of those dreams. It seems to me that the biggest challenges did not come from in-country experiences or people, but from fund-raising and dealing with leadership back home. As much patience as I developed for those from my new culture, I had a fraction of that forbearance when talking to friends back home. Perhaps I compared too much. The indigenous people, content in their tiny huts, seemed wiser than some wealthy and successful patrons back in my affluent homeland.

There are things that come along with the missionary's journey that don't fit every personality. I made myself at home in a sweaty, bug-infested hut in the Amazon jungle. Standing awkwardly in front of well-dressed church folks wasn't my forte. Throw in asking them for support ... my heart wasn't in it as time wore on.

The diminishing contribution levels and negativity of my sponsoring agency became a heavy weight on me, a black cloud that enveloped my faith. The authorities who sent me onto the mission field developed doubts because of my change in focus and due to the deteriorating bottom line. I prayed about the pay cut but did not know how to respond. At the same time, my direct communication pipeline to God the Father seemed to have switched to radio silence. Meanwhile, our friends in Peru and in the U.S. had conflicting advice.

Some of my missionary contemporaries around the world saw their support dollars rise exponentially as they founded orphanages and planted new churches. Jealousy wasn't the issue. Their accomplishments brought glory to God and spread His kingdom. We are all on the same team. The lack in my life seemed rooted in something else undefinable, but not in their success. Perhaps my benefactors would cure our financial woes if I explained our ministry better. Desperation lurked just around every corner, and the weight became too heavy for me to bear.

At one point, a U.S. pastor at a supporting church told me that our newsletters had gotten boring since I did not go out into the jungle anymore. "Maybe you should just get a regular job there in Peru," he said, trying to be helpful.

The jab landed like a friendly fire attack and drove me deeper into melancholy. I did not fault him and others like him, but neither did I take my hurt feelings to the Lord. Where, I wondered, might I find the place of forgiveness for my worsening attitudes when our bank account sits empty?

With a stiff upper lip, I sojourned on ... for a while. One glass of wine became two, and I had to admit to myself that alcohol again had taken hold of my life. The more the bills and troubles piled up, the more I sought escape and self-medication from my glass or two of wine per day.

As the snowball rolled downhill, it got bigger and bigger. With time, I had to tell my wife and the authorities back home that wine had gotten too much of a place in my life. This became my shipwreck. Alcohol had become a daily crutch. In my defense, I never missed a ministry event or counseling appointment because of wine. Somehow, Emma did not suspect a problem until I confessed.

Once my issue came to light with the mission board, everything came to a screeching halt. Those who had become less than encouraging back home used the occasion to suspend our ministry in Peru. I came forward, trying to be honest, seeking help, and I met closed hearts and slammed doors.

Once Emma and I returned to the U.S., the head of the mission board took me aside. "David, consider yourself on leave. The board needs to consider your future with our organization. Stay in the U.S. for now until I can call them together."

Frankly, the news shocked me. It looked like my time in Peru might end. Emma and I waited in limbo for two weeks until the board convened for their regular meeting. Stunned by the turn of events, both of us prayed with urgency and intensity. I tried to think positive thoughts. When we returned to Christian Assembly Church, we found only a little solace in the familiar faces there. I felt embarrassed by questions regarding our status. One brother asked me when we planned to head back to Peru. I responded, "I don't know." He did not press any further.

The mission board returned their decision. They canceled their association with us. Mercifully, they allowed Emma and me to return about a month later to say goodbye to our Peruvian church family. We also would use the time to close our house there, pick up our mementos, and fly home. The year 2013 brought news we would no longer be missionaries, at least for the foreseeable future. My heart broke, irreparably demolished beyond measure.

Like many who lose their ministry positions, my first thoughts centered on those we ministered to and the effects on them. Emma and I had grown to love so many people in Peru. We would not be seeing them. We would not share fellowship with our longtime church friends and co-laborers. Our lives would change in dramatic ways. I wept bitterly on multiple occasions.

While the decrease in contributions depressed me on the mission field, now I worried about all those who gave to us through the years. Would they understand how much they accomplished through our ministry? They didn't know all the people we helped, but our contributors deserve thanks on behalf of our clients. When any Christian gives to God's work, the Father rewards us in this present life and promises riches in heaven. I had to let go of my worries about our ministry partners and trust in the spiritual maturity of these benefactors.

Since our ministry focused on giving mercy to those in ministry, the church in Peru gave Emma and me double portions when we returned for that final visit. Their outpouring of love and concern salved our wounds and gave us hope. Tears flowed throughout our trip, and God used them to wash away many hurts. When the body of Christ operates as intended, we don't shoot our wounded. Brothers and sisters bear each other through life's turbulent times. We must lift up and help each other to continue on our journey.

*Redemption*
When things go wrong in life, we find out what we own. In my situation, my physical family stood by me through good times and bad. Emma needed time to process my indiscretions and the end of our missionary journey. Trust doesn't heal overnight, but she stayed by my side. She tried everything imaginable to help me heal, even as she also needed healing from the Lord.

We returned home to Virginia, not as victorious warriors, but as two broken people. While our identity should rest in Christ, not in a job, most men don't take job loss well. I had no identity left at all. Not that Christ took anything away, but it felt as if I gave up my sonship through my unfaithfulness. When missionaries, we came to speak at churches as honored guests. Now, we visited churches anonymously, hoping we might fit in somewhere. We became nobodies overnight, or at least we felt like it. A longtime Christian, I wondered if we would find any church fitting our situation.

Part of my recovery process involved admitting my addiction to alcohol. I used Alcoholics Anonymous (AA) to go through this process. The twelve steps brought comfort and showed me people much worse off than myself. The time-proven program of AA became useful in understanding my problems and solidifying my repentance. I found the meetings to be like church, only with cussing. We shared our hearts with each other, prayed the Lord's prayer, and trusted Him to rebuild our lives.

Some have said the doctrine of AA is like the plan of salvation, simplified for the alcohol-soaked mind and disguised for those angry at God. Although I never stooped to the lowest depths with my drinking, I knew wine had power over me. Vanquishing it forever from my life was the only option. Over the months ahead, I attended meetings, did not drink, worked the AA steps, and did the next right thing. Before I knew it, I found that I had been sober for a year.

Little by little, Emma and I rebuilt our lives. In some ways, it became like a wintertime turning to spring. As seasons progressed, so did our healing and God's redemption.

One grace in our lives involved our children. Fortunately, they had already reached adulthood as this trouble happened. They each moved forward with their own plans. Josh had joined the U.S. Marines before we moved back from Peru. Angela found her way to Liberty University and did well in school. Mary, our youngest, moved to Columbia, South Carolina where she worked and prepared to attend college in the fall.

Even in my early stages of restoration, I appreciated the Father's merciful timing for these life changes. The effects on our family might have been so much worse if all of it happened when the kids were living with us.

Although my identity as a missionary felt shaken, I worked on my identity as a son of God. I took one meager step toward the Heavenly Father and He came running in my direction. Although our road to redemption sometimes seemed long, I have had the best Father to help me through.

My love affair with Emma continued. She stood by me when some Delilah-types might have jumped ship during the stormy times. Sampson's hair grew back and so did my strength for ministry. We help struggling people at my local church. Emma and I also minister to those we meet outside the church walls, helping rebuild lives where we can.

My heart yearns to support missionaries and ministers. For now, Emma and I are active in our church's marriage and family ministry. The only drinking I do is drinking in God's love for us all. The experience sometimes leaves me tipsy in His Spirit, but never hung over.

When I think of Peru, my heart still aches a little. Memories lurk around every corner, triggered by the smallest things. Like a love affair recently ended, any small detail can conjure up a bittersweet memory. When I hear pouring rain, I remember lying alone in my tent in the rain forest. When we see someone dancing on a stage, the joy on the faces of the Shipibo dancers rekindles their energy as they unabashedly worshiped the Lord.

I still long for you, Peru, and I always will.

# Epilogue

Thanks for reading stories about our seventeen years on the mission field. My family and I experienced the richness of international culture, the blessing of a bicultural life, the joys and difficulties of foreign missions and the unforeseen struggles of re-entry into 'civilian' life. Since we left Peru, Emma and I enjoy a quieter existence in the Shenandoah Valley. My work as a cabinetmaker, gardener and church volunteer feels satisfying and peaceful. My wife enjoys the simple joys all around us, but she also works as an interpreter for nearby school systems, helping them bridge the gap with Spanish-speaking parents and children. We've had plenty of time to think about what happened and here are a few of the big lessons.

*Culture*
When asked to define culture, many of us struggle. Dictionary definitions prove incomplete and vague. For me, culture is the way we think and act based on expectations and standards learned from our family, friends and communities. Living among those from a different culture forces us to examine ourselves: our traditions, our habits and even our beliefs.

Latin American culture includes more protocol than we are used to in North America. Understanding their use of greetings and manners can speed up relationship development. They consider anything less than the expected greeting an affront and bad manners. At first, I found the formal hello and goodbye rituals cumbersome and a waste of time. Once used to the idea, the cordiality became a comfort. In North America, an all-business manner can lead to misunderstandings and uncertainties. Do I say hello here? Shake hands there? Hug? Say nothing the second time I pass by someone at work? My passport cultural education uncovered several gems that now benefit me often.

Cultural understanding breeds empathy. If we can overcome our immediate reaction that our way is the best way, it will open doors to new relationships for the gospel and for the betterment of our own lives. When my bent toward cultural superiority creeps into a conversation, I need look no farther than my wife's beautiful brown eyes. With a glance, she reminds me that humility looks better on me than arrogance.

*Bicultural Family*
By marrying a Peruvian, I permanently invited Peruvian culture into my life. Emma did the same with my American culture. We purposefully built our family based on both cultures. The heritage of our family shows up visibly and in more subtle ways.

Food is one noticeable benefit. Emma already knew how to cook Peruvian food when we got married, but she honed her skills on North America cuisine. When we lived with my parents for a year after our son was born, my mom took Emma under her wing and shared all the recipes and secrets she had accumulated over her years of cooking. While not as big of a contribution, my time in Cuba, Costa Rica, Ecuador, and Chile allowed me to add to our international repertoire of dishes.

Another benefit of our bi-cultural heritage is our children's fluency in Spanish and English. Once back in the States, they've received many opportunities personally and professionally thanks to the gift of two languages. When son Joshua turned three years old, he learned quickly that "quiero una galleta" would work a lot better than "I want a cookie" whenever Emma's parents were visiting.

Raising our family bilingually helped me maintain my Spanish as well and share language quirks I've noted from different countries. By talking over the complexity of words, God enriched our lives and helped us craft our sentences more precisely. We also mix and match words and phrases from English and Spanish. Sometimes we'll start a sentence in one language only to find the perfect word we need in another.

Along with these significant outward indicators of culture, our inward lives reflect both cultures. The Peruvian influence places a heavy emphasis on family but also on living in community with those connected to your family. Our children call the parents of their friends tía and tío, or aunt and uncle. We learned to extend our family to include treasured friends, a wonderful lesson from Peruvian culture. While valuing close relationships is not unique to Peru, the use of these names points to that value in a more obvious way. Our children grew up cherishing friends as extended family. In a world where people often become isolated, we all could learn from the practice of widening our family circle.

By relocating to Peru, our children found a richness and diversity of culture that they would have never known had we stayed in the U.S. All three children became immersed in Peruvian culture and understand it far better than mere book knowledge. Living in Peru gave them thousands of opportunities unknown to children of only one culture. They've grown up with the ability to recognize that different does not mean wrong. They have a certain adaptability that comes with a broader view of the world.

These advantages are serving each child well as they make their way in the world. Josh is now a captain in the Marine Corps. He understands cultural differences among his fellow Marines which helped him flourish as a leader and friend. Angela has a heart for missionary kids and wants to be in a position where she can support them. Her experience gives her ample opportunities to work in the U.S. and internationally. Mary credits her background as her inspiration for learning more languages and being interested in public relations and interpreting. She also finds that her cross-cultural background allows her to adapt to diverse work environments. All three of our children have been able to use their command of Spanish to open doors while they've been back in the U.S.

*Missionary Life*
God is a faithful provider. I have so many stories that would encourage almost anyone to become a missionary. However, we faced plenty of hardships and difficulties. No matter the quality of pre-deployment training, the reality of missions work never perfectly matches expectations. Most of us are optimistic. Foreign missions almost require an entrepreneurial personality. By the time you head out to your assignment, you may have prayed and fasted for months or years. You probably studied and gave a hundred presentations about your plans and dreams. You believe that the entire experience will be the best years of your life. And it might turn out that way.

Your ministry may flourish and produce almost instant results. Hundreds may come to Christ in the first few months. In the first year, God may miraculously heal a leper colony and you may eradicate poverty for an entire people group. Even better, all of your shortcomings and character defects might disappear the minute you touch down on foreign soil. Surly loners may become happy extroverts and lazy procrastinators may suddenly become industrious church planters.

Everything may be bliss from the outset, but more likely you find yourself with a series of successes and failures. You may find that your expectations were far from the daily reality of scratching out a new field work. Missionary success is a marathon no matter how we try to sprint. It may take months and years to build the ministry of your dreams or, more precisely, God's plan.

Once on the field, reality smacks us in the face. Ministry is hard work and things seldom go according to our best laid plans. Our weaknesses become magnified in difficult, unfamiliar circumstances. Flawed human beings under tremendous stress sometimes break. Unreasonably high expectations of ourselves, fellow workers or a spouse can lead to disappointment. Remain humble and don't think the work you are doing is more important than someone else's vocation. The best preparation for the mission field is to develop reasonable expectations, patience and trust in the Lord.

*Pastoral Care and Member Care*
I am so grateful for the support we received from our missionary pastor, Phillip Miles. Located back in the US, Pastor Phillip comforted us through many trials and frequently gave us wise advice. His pastoral care often sustained us. Our sending church pastors and supporters also prayed for us and sent us much-needed notes of encouragement, particularly in those early years. We know that many of these folks had their hands full with their own church responsibilities. In retrospect, we wouldn't expect people back home to be a constant source of encouragement when we are thousands of miles away. They have their own issues. You must build your

own support network, probably within your new country.

Beyond pastoral care and Christian fellowship, missionaries need a special help we called member care. As a missionary, you are part of a special fraternity/sorority with specific needs. I firmly believe that member care for missionaries is best accomplished by those trained or experienced in this specialized field. When confronted with the futility of trying to be the perfect missionary, we must bring our shortcomings to the cross. If not careful, we won't realize the mental and emotional strain we have been under until the toll becomes too great. A few years after we settled into missionary work, we recognized the need for our own member care. A friendly voice back home can make all the difference in relieving stress and suggesting healthy perspectives on our vitally important work.

Our desire to see pastors and missionaries in Peru receive member support fueled a major change to our missionary focus. Let me emphasize: Missionaries serve behind enemy lines and desperately need professional backup. Without help, we can become sitting ducks for heartache and shipwreck!

*Independent or Missionary Organization*
Emma and I accepted our commission onto the mission field through a loose network of independent churches. Not being part of a major denomination, we felt this organization best fit our needs. They collected our support, did the bookkeeping and paid us each month. They helped with minimal human resources services. We looked to them for our spiritual covering and answered to them for church discipline.

Once on the field, we doubted our choice of sending organizations. Frankly, we could have used better continuing education training, more help with fund-raising/donor care and additional pastoral support on the ground in Peru.

If you are considering a long-term assignment, look around

and research the options. Weigh pros and cons of various organizations. Think about the services provided, safety nets in place and your own tolerance for bureaucracy.

Missionaries sometimes joke that when someone in an established denomination expresses an interest in missions, their leader pulls out the 300-page manual of things this person needs to accomplish before being sent. Those from an unaffiliated church might get a different reaction. "Great! When can you leave?" Throughout the years, we tried to find a different sending agency. We never found one that seemed a proper fit. Plus, in retrospect, the freedom of being more independent is hard to give up.

*Fundraising*
Raising support is often the elephant in the room. It influences many aspects of missionary life. Choosing a lifestyle financed by the giving of others comes with baggage. Unless you know a lot of very wealthy people, it will mean financial sacrifices for you and your entire family. Some choices were difficult on our hearts, like when we couldn't afford for all of us to return to the States for my mother's funeral.

Be careful not to develop an unhealthy attitude toward your work. Although all Christians should be excellent stewards of their resources, God doesn't intend for us on the mission field to become workaholics or guilt-ridden over every purchase. Without a clear and healthy view of self and the costs of ministry, it may feel like a never-ending need for to justify our support. We sometimes took it personally when contributions dropped off. I thought maybe I wasn't doing an adequate job at this facet of being a missionary.

However, even with the awkwardness of asking for money, living on a tight budget, and other uncomfortable aspects of funds raising, we cannot deny the joys of foreign ministry life. When we began fundraising, we slept in hotels and ate at restaurants while we traveled from one church to another. At first, we knew no one well enough to garner invitations to stay in private homes. This got old quickly and proved expensive. Once we established liaisons with the churches and families we visited, people invited us to stay with them. It became a huge blessing to develop close friendships with fellow believers. These brothers and sisters in Christ proved some of the sweetest people we met, many of whom still keep in touch.

Once on the field, we returned to the States once a year to visit our supporters and try to make new friends. Long car rides led to boredom, but also to excellent adventures. We met people and went places we would never had known had we not been missionaries. Even though the term working vacation elicited groans from our kids, they remember many treasured moments as well. One year, someone gave us coupons to various attractions in Myrtle Beach, SC. We stayed several days, enjoying a water park, Ripley's aquarium and the Dixie Stampede. Another year, we found ourselves in a giant corn maze in Lancaster, PA while visiting my nephew and his family.

Imagine my terror the first time (as part of a missions conference in Florida) we rode roller coasters. Even in my native Washington, D.C. region, we enjoyed sightseeing and touring the Smithsonian museums. Saints opened their hearts and their homes in total generosity. A lump in my throat reminds me of all the love we shared over our missionary journey.

The hours together bound my wife and I to our three children. We built a ministry together. Our family stayed tight through thick and thin. Each year, I carefully crafted my missions message to share with our supporting churches. As we traveled, the kids soon knew my spiel verbatim. Josh helped by critiquing my presentations. I had my own, built in speaking coach! I fondly remember once when he said,

"Dad, you know that one joke you tell? I think you should take that out of your message ... you're the only person who laughs at it." He was right.

Having to raise our own support gave us an opportunity to learn to live with little money. When Emma and I moved back to Peru, we brought what fit in 13 suitcases. Our first Christmas tree in Peru consisted of a hand-drawn picture taped to the wall. Personally, I loved the irony, but Emma and the kids weren't too keen on our virtual tree. I found something freeing about living with few possessions. The Lord provided our needs. Our family never went hungry. Sure, sometimes things were tight, but these precious times afforded ample opportunities to ramp up our trust in Him.

*Re-Entry*
One of the most difficult parts of being a missionary is when it is all over and it's time to return to your passport country permanently. They call this expatriate re-entry. Some may think we'd be excited to come home, but Peru felt like home for so long. Leaving our place of ministry became harder than anyone could imagine. As missionaries, we put all our eggs in God's basket. We quit our jobs, sold our house and set sail with the idea we would serve on the field forever. We devised no plan B. We worked hard at adapting to and falling in love with Peruvian culture and tons of new people. We became intentional about building long-term relationships, not only with our target people group, but with supporters back in the U.S.

Once the dreaded moment arrives to return, a part of our heart stayed planted in Peru. We experienced a tremendous void once occupied by ministry and Peruvian friends. This season felt like a bone-dry desert. The Lord ministered to our hearts during this grieving period. We longed for Peru and our old life. We felt like fish out of water in the U.S.

When overflowing with stories and experiences, our practice had been to tour churches and share with others. Now, that platform disappeared. We missed the opportunities that had once been plentiful. Despite the emotional challenges, God met us in our times of prayer and devotion. The changes strengthened our relationships with Him and with our U.S. family. Jesus cleansed me of hidden pride and showed me how much I have in common with all believers. Stepping down from the pedestal of the title missionary, I found deeper fellowship with brothers and sisters.

What have I learned? Despite my weaknesses, the Lord used me for 17 years as a messenger, and He will continue to use this broken vessel. I'm moved by a picture of a Japanese vase, damaged and repaired with gold to fill the cracks. Yes, I was an accidental missionary. I became the richest man in the world by awakening to hear and follow His voice. I found a Peruvian princess who said yes to life with this gringo and blessed me with three wonderful children. I fell in love with a country that embraced me and made me one of its own. The process broke me, but the Lord continues to refill the voids with His golden healing. Thank you for helping in my recovery by reading this book about Him.

*More About David L. Winters*

Author David L. Winters spent 34 years working for the federal government, including the last ten with the U.S. Department of Homeland Security. Following his retirement in 2016, he became a full-time writer and speaker. David has an MBA (2003) from Regent University and a B.A. in Journalism (1981) from The Ohio State University. After living in Ohio, Oklahoma City and Chicago, he moved to the Washington, D.C. suburbs in 1989 and continues to live there. He is available for speaking engagements and can be contacted through his website: www.sabbaticalofthemind.net.

**Other Titles by David L. Winters:**

Taking God to Work: *The Keys to Ultimate Success*
Sabbatical of the Mind: *The Journey from Anxiety to Peace*
Driver Confessional

www.ingramcontent.com/pod-product-compliance
Lightning Source LLC
Chambersburg PA
CBHW020254030426
42336CB00010B/762